GOLDIE

GOLDIE

THE MAN AND HIS MOVIES

ANITAA PADHYE

Translated from the Marathi by Vikrant Pande

AMARYLLIS

AMARYLLIS
An imprint of Manjul Publishing House Pvt. Ltd.
• 7/32, Ansari Road, Daryaganj, New Delhi 110 002
Website: www.manjulindia.com
Registered Office:
• 10, Nishat Colony, Bhopal 462 003 – India

First published in 2020

ISBN 978-93-90085-62-0

Translated from the Marathi by Vikrant Pande

Printed and bound in India by Replika Press Pvt Ltd.

From the Heart

On the morning of 23 February, 2004, I received the news that Goldie was admitted to Lilavati Hospital in critical condition after a heart attack. I was shocked. Not only had I known Goldie for many years, I was writing a book on him. But before I could even leave for the hospital, his PRO called and said, 'He is no more!'

I didn't have the courage to visit the hospital or go for his cremation, remaining restless and shocked the whole day. A few journalists called up to interview me because of my book on Goldie, but I was in no mood to talk to them.

I attended the fourth day function at the Arya Samaj hall in Santacruz. Dev Anand and other family members conducted the rituals. After the ceremony, as everyone streamed out, I went near the stage to look at a large photograph of Goldie. I touched it and the tears, frozen within me, started to flow. His smile was permanently fixed in the picture. I somehow managed to stop my tears, spoke a few words to the staff of Ketnav Theatre and stepped out.

That night I sobbed like a child. Memories flooded my mind.

In 1992, I used to work for a Hindi film weekly and was asked to interview Goldie, aka Vijay Anand. When I phoned him to request an interview, I received a very cold response,

'No! What is the point of the interview? I am not doing anything these days.'

'It's about your work in the film industry.'

'Call me after fifteen days,' he said and hung up.

When I called him after a fortnight, he once again excused himself and asked me to call later.

Had it been anyone else but Goldie, it might have been tempting to drop the interview itself. But my deep respect for his films and my persistence paid off after five or six attempts.

I finally reached his home in the building that housed Ketnav Studios. I felt as if I was meeting a long-lost friend. He received me warmly. Before I could begin, he almost interviewed me, asking me about my career, my family etc. When I told him my full name, he asked whether I was the same person against whom Dev Anand had filed a case. I nodded; Dev Anand had filed a defamation case against me and my editor for ₹1 crore! The case was sub judice at that time.

I had told the truth, and wondered whether Goldie would ask me to get out! But to my surprise he said, 'Come on, let's begin the interview. Ask what you wish to.'

This was my first meeting. He spoke so endearingly that I felt as if I had known him for a long time.

'Anitaa, I don't know why but I like talking to you. I can feel the vibrations when the wavelengths match,' Goldie said, putting his palm on his wrist.

I met him a few more times, and each time our relationship deepened. I had not met a man so simple, straightforward, direct and warm. He did not behave in a *filmy* manner despite being in the industry for decades.

No longer a reporter and a film director talking, we started to meet as friends. It was then that I decided to write his life story. He agreed to my proposal. He had always stayed away from the press and media, and was surprised that someone was keen to tell his story. 'You write well,' he said, 'and the best part is I like telling you about my life, I don't know why.'

Goldie spoke the way he wrote a screenplay, describing the smallest of events. He did not deviate from the topic or ramble. I would often record what he said and Goldie would be upset if someone disturbed him while we were at work. I realized this when I once took my niece with me. Goldie was not in his element that day. He said, 'Anitaa, I don't know why I open up to you. But I am not comfortable when someone else is around.'

He had often mentioned that the only person – other than his wife Sushma – with whom he had been so candid and open about himself and his work – was me.

Goldie was a sensitive soul and would sob like a child while narrating some incidents from his life. At the same time, he would show childlike excitement and enthusiasm while talking about a particular script or the kind of efforts he put into a movie. He would literally relive the moments.

Goldie taught me a lot of things. I wasn't shabby in my appearance, but I had never given much thought to putting on makeup. But Goldie told me, 'Anitaa, you are a pretty girl and you should make yourself presentable. He would explain about pedicure and manicure, about hairstyles and what lipstick colour would suit me. He taught me a lot about changing myself, not just outwardly but from inside. I had philosophy as a subject in college, but Goldie had done intense research in that field. We would discuss such topics for hours together. He taught me how to direct my thoughts. He helped me with my self-confidence.

Our birthdays were a week apart and we never forgot them. If I didn't call him on his birthday in the morning itself, he would call me in the evening and say, 'Looks like you were busy. I was waiting for your call since morning.'

We loved to debate on various issues. At times I would say, putting my point across firmly, 'Goldie sahab, you have to agree. I am, after all, eight days older than you.' We would both laugh at that.

He taught me, among many things, that one can change one's destiny, albeit a little. He firmly believed that a man had the capability to do so if he put in sincere efforts.

He had studied astrology and palmistry deeply. Whatever he predicted about me turned out true. We believe there is a child in each one of us, but I always saw a mature man in

Goldie. Very few people are truly able to understand another person – Goldie was one of them. At one stage, I had left a job because of disgusting office politics. A lot of people criticized my decision, except Goldie, who fully supported me.

It was while I was working on the book that Goldie suffered his first heart attack. I was not able to work on the book while he was hospitalized and later when he was recuperating at home. Once he recovered, he started working on the movie, *Jana Na Dil Se Door.* He had many reasons, I feel, to engage in such a project. He wanted to make the movie as homage to his brother, Chetan Anand. Goldie had promised a producer and had written the script before he fell ill. He spent ten to twelve hours a day to complete the script in a forthnight. But, unfortunately, the producer did not show any interest. All the trouble Goldie had taken were wasted, leaving him upset.

Goldie was much senior to me in age and experience but would consult me for his film, discussing the casting and other such things. I had suggested Aamir Khan as the lead, as I liked his dedication to a project. But for various reasons they never discussed the movie and Goldie cast newcomers. Goldie suffered a lot while making the movie and had to overcome many obstacles. Unfortunately, the movie has never been released till date.

When Goldie's son Vaibhav wanted to enter the film industry as a director, Goldie had asked me for my opinion on which director he should be an apprentice to.

He would share everything with me. On his 25th wedding anniversary, he called me and said in his usual style, 'Anitaa, Goldie here. We are going out for dinner to celebrate our 25th anniversary. I thought I will tell you.'

He was a transparent soul and I never felt any discrepancy between his words and deeds. A lot of people who seem very respectable in the first few meetings show their true colours after a while. But Goldie was never two-faced. I found him to be the same in the twelve years of my association with him. I have so many memories of him, it would make another book.

Despite the age difference between us, he was more like a friend to me and I could speak openly on any subject. After completing the book, I had called Goldie. It was a week before his death. I wanted to clarify a few things about some films.

'Anitaa, I am not well but we will surely meet next week. I am committed to the book. Please be assured.'

He had always kept his word – except this last one!

It has been a long time since Goldie died, but I continue to speak to him in my mind. His death was a great personal loss to me. He was someone who understood me well, gave me right advice, and loved me without any selfish motives. He was a true friend to me.

I had faced a lot of difficulties while writing this book and almost gave up many times, but for Goldie's sake I had to complete the book. Despite making many artistic movies and some landmark ones like *Guide* in the Indian film industry, Goldie never received the kind of accolades he should have. Some newspapers merely said, 'ex censor board chairman Vijay Anand died'. What a tragedy that he should be known for his chairmanship of the censor board! Some newspapers, while talking of his movies, wrongly mentioned *Kala Pani* and *Paying Guest* as movies directed by him. They had no knowledge about Goldie and his work. Probably, they were not interested in a non-glamourous personality like Goldie. Newspapers and television channels were giving more footage to Raveena Tandon's wedding. I felt it was my duty to tell the readers what an intelligent, sensitive and great filmmaker Goldie was.

I hope you will love this book, too.

Anitaa Padhye

An extraordinary filmmaker, an accomplished dialogue writer, and an ingenious storyteller, all rolled into one – that's Goldie, aka Vijay Anand, for you. Rarely does one find a personality from the film industry who is not *filmy*. It wouldn't be wrong to say, however, that despite his vast contribution to the film industry, Goldie remains largely ignored.

Goldie was born on 22 January, 1935. in Gurdaspur, Punjab, bordering Pakistan. His father, Pishorimal Anand, was a lawyer, who also knew eight classical languages, including Sanskrit, Greek, Farsi and Hebrew. Because of him, Goldie learnt the *choupai*, quatrain verse, from *Ramcharitmanas* by-heart when still a child.

When Pishorimal's first wife died during childbirth, he married her sister. They had eight children: Savitri, Chetan, Kanta, Sheela, Dev, Usha, Lata, and, the youngest, Vijay. With his golden hair and fair skin, Vijay soon became 'Goldie'. The siblings did not live together too long. Chetan, 20 years older than Goldie, went to England for higher studies, where he lived for about four years and worked for the BBC. He was Bhappa, 'elder brother' in Punjabi, to his siblings, and Dev, was Papa. With two sisters studying in Lahore, the only children staying with their mother were Dev, Goldie and the two younger sisters.

The apple of his mother's eye, Goldie grew up seeing her being treated by various allopathic doctors, *vaids,* and an occasional homeopath, due to her deteriorating health. While there was no cure for her condition, she may improve if taken to a hill station, the doctors suggested. Pishorimal would take her and the children to the Summer Resort Lodge in Dalhousie. Dev took care of his mother, getting the prescribed goat's milk for her daily. On her deathbed, she blessed Dev, that he would earn a lot of fame – words that turned out to be prophetic.

Worried about her children's future, she ensured that they had everything they needed, visiting Lahore to buy shoes, socks and clothes for them. Goldie didn't remember his mother ever shouting, getting angry or raising her voice. It was her quiet nature that Goldie recalled whenever he thought of her.

In the absence of the eldest brother, Chetan, who was in England by then, the domestic responsibilities fell upon Dev. Goldie, ten years his junior, was his favourite sibling, and they often walked hand in hand. They would purchase a basket of mangoes and leave it in a flowing river for cooling. Goldie was constantly amazed at his brother's ingenuity.

Kanta, Goldie's older sister, lived in Lahore after marriage. Within two years of her marriage, their mother's condition worsened. She was restless, wondering who would take care of Goldie after her death. Kanta assured her, while visiting her from Lahore once, 'Ma, don't worry. We are here, aren't we?'

Not only did Kanta nurse her mother in Gurdaspur, she took Goldie with her to Lahore. Six-year-old Goldie joined a school in Lahore.

A few months later he heard Kanta's father-in-law speak to her husband, Chaman, and handing him a telegram. Kanta's crying was immediately audible. The young boy sensed it was bad news, though he could not imagine what. Kanta called Goldie to her room and said,

'Dear, our mother has been taken away by God in a golden chariot.'

'Will she never return?'

'No. Never,' Kanta said, trying to make her young brother understand.

Goldie did not cry, remaining quiet. They arrived at Gurdaspur to find a crowd outside their house. In a window on the first floor, Goldie could see men and women crying.

He waved excitedly to his nanny, wondering why she was so sad. He returned to Lahore after his mother's funeral, but came back to Gurdaspur later.

In the meanwhile, Chetan had returned from England. Soon thereafter, he married Uma Chatterjee, who had embraced Christianity. Uma's father was the vice-chancellor of Lahore University. Chetan was his favourite student and they played tennis together. While studying, Chetan and Uma participated in plays and debates. The friendship soon blossomed into love. Chetan had managed to tell his ailing mother about Uma through Kanta. But he had not dared confess to his father, knowing well he would never accept a Christian daughter-in-law. Chetan had his mother's support, who had only one condition – that his wife, whoever she may be, should look after his siblings. On her deathbed she even extracted a promise from her husband that he would welcome any girl Chetan married.

Respecting his promise to her, Chetan's father did not oppose the marriage, though he refused to attend the wedding in Lahore, upset that he had not been consulted. Chetan had told Uma of his mother's wish and, thus, when he got a job in the prestigious Doon School, they took Goldie with them. Goldie spent a part of his childhood there.

The Doon school, with its English-speaking students, gave Goldie an inferiority complex. The students, while respectfully wishing Chetan 'good morning', sniggered at Goldie's poor English. Goldie could read Hindi and, at the mere age of seven, had not only read the *Ramayan,* which he had carried from Gurdaspur, but also the *Mahabharat,* which he found in the school's library. Chetan had not admitted Goldie in the school as he was not sure of the boy's future plans.

Chetan continued with his love for the theatre by performing for the All India Radio. Soon, he was attracted to the upcoming medium of cinema. He started studying the art and immersed himself in writing a script. At the same time, he engaged in discussions with a German scholar, reading books like *Russian Theory* and *Wood of Queen* on cinema. Chetan was keen to move to Bombay to try his hand at production and acting. He had taken a few scripts to Bombay but had not received any encouraging response. He moved to Bombay to try his luck while Goldie and Uma returned to Lahore.

❖❖❖

Landing in Bombay, Chetan met his college friend Balraj Sahni, who had become an actor, and they both started visiting the Indian Peoples Theatre Association (IPTA).

Dev, too, had moved to Bombay to try his luck in films. His father, whose business was not doing well by then, was keen for him to pursue his M.A. and work in a bank. Dev had no interest in taking up a mundane job and, one day, simply packed a few clothes and landed in Bombay with ₹20 in his pocket. He stayed with Chetan's friend Raja Rao, a famous writer, and Khwaja Ahmad Abbas, a newspaper columnist. To make ends meet, he joined the Military Censor office as a clerk for ₹85 a month. Dev did not like the idea of reading someone else's letters one bit but had no choice. The job of the censor office was to delete any war-related information in the letters sent by the soldiers during the World War II period. Dev's job was to read the letters before forwarding them.

Chetan 'Bhappa' and Dev 'Papa' were in Bombay while young Goldie continued his studies in Lahore. The medium of teaching in the schools in Lahore was Urdu. A tutor was appointed for Goldie to learn Urdu, but everything changed the day they decided to move to Bombay.

The question regarding Goldie's school admission arose. Chetan was staying in Pali Hill, Bandra. They wanted Goldie to study in a Hindi-medium school, lest he forgot the language. But there were only two such schools: the Marwari Mahavidyalaya in Churchgate and the Poddar School in Santacruz. Goldie joined the Poddar School, which was not far off.

Goldie was fond of his sister-in-law, Uma, and started addressing her as didi. Chetan was busy with his plays and writing, while Dev was struggling with his job and finding a place in the film world. Uma continued to look after Goldie as if he were her own son.

Uma worked in *The Illustrated Weekly* magazine and Chetan was a news reader on radio. He became friends with Pandit Ravi Shankar, the sitar maestro, Ali Akbar Khan, the sarod player, and Pannalal Ghosh, the brilliant flautist. Even as Chetan indulged in plays and read news, his first love remained film direction. He finally found an opportunity in 1945 to direct the movie *Neecha Nagar*. The movie starred Kamini Kaushal, Uma Anand and Rafique Anwar, with Ravi Shankar as the music director. It was the first Indian movie to win an award at the France Film Festival, but barely created a ripple at the box office.

Chetan's house was literally a lodge for people struggling to make a mark in the film world and on stage. He had started a theatre group, Hind Manch and play rehearsals took place at his home. Goldie, all of ten, was given the task of 'prompting' and executed his job diligently. During those days, Balraj Sahni and his wife were staying at Chetan's house. Even Zohra Sehgal, the famous actor and dance director from the Uday Shankar school and attached to Prithvi Theatre, stayed at Chetan's house with her husband and actor Kameshwar Sehgal. Not to mention Rafique Anwar Ahmad and Rashid Anwar, who were regular visitors!

They all met Goldie; modest, innocent, intelligent Goldie. Most would lose to him in a game of chess. Kameshwar Sehgal and Hamid Bhatt openly praised him, calling him the most intelligent amongst the three brothers. Goldie himself was unaffected by all this praise. In awe of Chetan's brilliance and an admirer of Dev's's handsome 'film-star' looks, he took such compliments lightly. So there he was, growing up in a house full of artistic minds, and settled well in his school. He walked and then took a bus and a train to school; the train pass cost him ₹2 and his school fees were ₹4 a month. He would get 4 annas each day; 2 for the bus and 2 as pocket money! School was from quarter to eleven till 4 p.m. He would have an early lunch and leave for school; Uma would prepare something for him when he returned. Goldie was not particularly fond of the school as it did not have a playground and there were no extra-curricular activities. Thanks to his teacher, Mohan ji, he was learning Hindi well though. Goldie was Mohan ji's favourite student; Goldie always knew the answer when others didn't.

Goldie's best friend, Sushil Nivetia, lived in Khar. Those days, there were rice fields around Khar Ghymkhana. Goldie and Sushil would visit Gymkhana sometimes to enjoy a *batata vada,* which cost an anna each. Goldie would walk all the way from Santacruz to Pali Hill to save money for the snack.

Goldie was a shy student and, despite the school being a co-ed one, never spoke to girls. Sujata, with her high marks in Sanskrit, was Goldie's informal competitor; she came first and Goldie second in class. The two never spoke to each other, not even a hello.

He met her many years later at a party organized by the Governor. For a moment he wondered why she seemed familiar – and then it dawned on him that she was Sujata from his class. Goldie, gathering some courage, asked,

'Are you Sujata?'

She smiled. 'Yes! Are you Vijay?'

'Yes,' Goldie replied.

'You have done very well.'

'You, too, have done well,' Goldie reciprocated.

Sujata Manohar was a famous high-court judge by then. They both had earned a name for themselves in their respective fields and felt a camaraderie.

Vishwanath, another schoolmate, was a playwright. It was in his play that Goldie got a chance to showcase his acting talent. Goldie had no plans of acting but Vishwanath pushed Goldie on to the stage while the play was going on. Goldie's brother was an actor, so he can act too, was the general feeling. A nervous Goldie did his best, and was shocked when everyone praised him. Instead of using high-flown and ornamental Hindi,

Vishwanath should have used simple, colloquial language in his plays, was all Goldie said. Another close friend of Goldie's was Shyam Yedekar. The three of them studied together in St. Xavier's College.

The bond between Goldie and Dev, already established in Gurdaspur, strengthened further in Bombay. Dev never scolded Goldie, but did strike him once.

The fuse blew at home one day and Goldie volunteered to repair it, though Dev recommended getting an electrician. The whole house soon plunged into darkness. An incensed Dev Anand slapped Goldie hard. But that was the only time. Dev and Goldie – who shared a room most of the time as there were always some guests in the house – were like-minded, but different from the other family members. The key reason for this was Goldie's upbringing. Uma had a western background; Goldie's father was immersed in Indian culture. Goldie was confused listening to Uma discuss Socrates, Plato, Aristotle, Einstein and Russian cinema. Chetan, too, was largely into western thought though he had studied in a gurukul. He had become half a Britisher having lived in England for a few years. He had also studied in Lahore University, not to mention the influence of Uma's side of the family. Dev really understood Goldie. On returning from the censor office, Dev would find Goldie waiting for him at the Pali Hill bus stop. They would have a cup of tea at the Irani tea stall nearby, buy Parle-G biscuits and an occasional packet of Polson Butter. Dev was too lean those days and working out at home to improve his physique He was told to have butter regularly, so the brothers enjoyed a butter sandwich now and then.

Time passed by. Goldie graduated to higher classes while Dev still waited for success despite having done a few films. With Bombay Talkies' *Ziddi,* Dev was finally on his way to stardom.

Dev and co-star Suraiya's love affair began on the sets of the film *Vidya,* shot in 1948. Actresses Kamini Kaushal and Durga Khote, and cameraman Dwarka Dive would help the couple meet in secret, away from her grandmother's eye. Suraiya would shower her love on the young Goldie, who had started referring to her as Suraiya bhabi. The Anands were not opposed to the marriage. Till the end Goldie believed that had Dev Papa got married to Suraiya, he would have been a different person and achieved greater heights of success.

❖❖❖

Chetan contemplated quitting the industry when *Neecha Nagar* failed, but Dev did not like the fact that his brother was depressed. He decided to start his own production house with Chetan in 1949. That year Uma had given birth to a baby boy, Ketan; the production house was named Navketan Films, keeping in mind the arrival of the next generation. Chetan had started an acting academy at Khira Nagar, Santacruz, with the help of Balraj Sahni, Ramesh Sehgal and others, but the venture did not do well and had to be wound up. This space was used as Naveketan's office. The first movie from the production house was *Afsar,* starring Dev and Suraiya, but it bombed at the box office, leaving Chetan shattered. Dev, however, was determined to continue, and gave Guru Dutt, a friend working at Prabhat Studios as a dance director, an opportunity to direct *Baazi.*

At that time Goldie had finished school and joined St. Xavier's College near Churchgate. With his love for languages, he chose to do a degree in Arts.

Ameen Sayani, later famous as a radio jockey, was Goldie's classmate, and acted in plays, while his elder brother, Hamid Sayani, was a famous stage artist who visited Xavier's to direct plays. Farukh Mehta and Farokh Engineer, who later became famous stars in cinema and cricket, were Goldie's contemporaries. Students of Xavier's were not fond of watching Hindi movies, so no one really knew Goldie as Dev Anand's brother.

The first year was hard on Goldie and he felt as if he had come into a different school rather than a college. Barring a few, all others were from an English-medium background and spoke the language fluently, behaving like British gentlemen. They all looked like Christians and the atmosphere, too, was similar; Goldie, with his Hindi-medium background, felt like a fish out of water, and was also bullied.

Gathering a few friends and a lot of courage, Goldie decided to stage a play in the first year. He was initially nervous – but the moment he stepped on stage, he was filled with confidence.

Goldie and his friends decided to stage Hindi plays even though it was not easy to find boys who spoke Hindi well and could act. One day, while having tea in the college canteen, he asked a boy called Mahendra if he would act in a play. The boy smiled and replied that he had never acted on stage.

Goldie explained his problem. He knew that Mahendra sang on stage so didn't have stage fright. He was sure he could be made to act too. The boy would later be known as the famous playback singer, Mahendra Kapoor!

Slowly but surely Goldie was able to collect a group of boys and formed a theatre group, Hindi Vidyarthi Mandal. They needed girls to act in the play but Goldie was shy to ask them. Goldie's sister, Usha, was in Xavier's and joined the group.

Finally, a few girls did join the group, with those who did not act helping in the costume section.

Once Goldie asked an Anglo-Indian girl if she would be willing to act in his Hindi plays. She snubbed him, saying, 'What nonsense? I don't speak Hindi. I speak Hindi only with my servant.'

Goldie was nonplussed, but he later used her sentence, 'I speak Hindi only with my servant,' in one of his plays, getting a lot of claps.

Goldie's group was in place, but choosing the play was the problem. He had tried Jayshankar's play in the first year, but the ornamental language was not appealing. He had heard, in his childhood, the simple language used by Chetan and his group. He believed a play should have simple, conversational language. All the scripts he went through sounded bombastic. Finally, Goldie decided to write his own play.

The play *Rehearsal* was about that – the rehearsals for a play, and the mishaps that occur during rehearsing. It was an experimental play during those times. Goldie played the role of the director, guiding and directing the actors. He would go and sit amongst the audience while directing them on stage, all part of the play itself. His sister Usha and Mahendra Kapoor were the lead pair.

The play was selected for the inter-college competition among 25 others. The judges consisted of famous producer-director Ramanand Sagar, actor Premnath and Haldikar, a well-known Marathi stage actor. The judges were impressed. They had not seen a play of this kind. Despite being a play, the treatment was cinematic with elements of realism and natural acting. The play presented by K.C. College had a huge set with lighting et al and was a clear contender for the first prize. But Goldie's *Rehearsal* bagged the honours. Not just that, Mahendra Kapoor was judged the best actor.

Naturally, the students of K.C. College were not amused, and complained that Goldie had won the award because he was Dev Anand's brother. They threw eggs and tomatoes at Premnath in protest when he came on stage to give the award. Without flinching, Premnath addressed the students, 'You may throw tomatoes and eggs at me, but I want to tell you the reason why we chose Vijay Anand's play as the winner. The three of us, the judges, are all experienced in our fields. I predict that this boy will one day become an excellent director and actor. You are young and may not realize that today, but the boy has talent which will shine one day. It is an opinion we all share.'

Goldie had seen Premnath at Prithvi Theatre, where Chetan used to act.

The play was then selected for an inter-university competition in Delhi, with 37 plays competing for the top slot. Goldie's play won the top honours and the special evening show was to be attended by none other than Prime Minister Jawaharlal Nehru.

Goldie and his team were excited. That afternoon they

visited Connaught Place and had lassi. Soon their stomachs started rumbling and they suffered from loose motions. Medicines were of no use. They were wondering how they would put up the play when an idea struck Goldie. He told everyone, 'If anyone wants to use the toilet, he or she should exit saying, "I will be back in a minute".' The theme of the play was rehearsals, so the line did not look out of place. Nehru and the audience assumed that it was a part of the play and were amused. Despite winning the competition at Delhi, Goldie did not receive any praise at St. Xavier's College. There were no congratulatory messages from the principal. But Goldie cocked a snook at everyone by rewriting the play into a satire. Meanwhile, Goldie and Mahendra Kapoor had become good friends. It was Goldie who suggested to Mahendra that he should stop copying Mohammed Rafi and develop his own singing style. Goldie, Mahendra Kapoor, Sushil Nivetia, Kapil Mehra, Devendra Chopra, Dharamveer, Satyadev Dubey, Usha, Kareem Lakdawala and others were now a group. Another one-act play by Goldie, *Three Goons,* also won an award for the best play.

The story of *Three Goons* was about three people who were released from jail and decided to loot a house, only to discover the goodness of the people staying there despite facing many problems in life. The goons realize that looting and stealing were not the right way to live. If the family in that home could walk on the right path despite all odds, why couldn't they? The goons have a change of heart and decide to help the family, becoming good citizens along the way. (The Marathi film, *We Are Going to our Village,* has a similar story.) The three goons in Goldie's play were enacted by Mahendra Kapoor, Wasi Khan and Satyadev Dubey.

Goldie had established his unique style of simple, straightforward dialogues. The Hindi professors at Xavier's, Mr. Prabhat and Mr. Methani, encouraged Goldie.

Goldie wrote, directed and acted in nearly 20-odd plays during his college days. He had realized that there was a lot of difference between literary writing and a play or a film script. His family background in films had influenced his plays. He used minimum dialogue, natural expressions, and an easy flow of events with story-telling. It would make spectators feel that an incident was unfolding right before their eyes. Goldie was encouraged a lot by Uma didi who would attend his rehearsals and give suggestions.

Goldie had now completed his first year of B.A.

❖❖❖

Aandhiyan was being produced under the Navketan banner, with Ali Akbar Khan as the music director. Chetan, keen for Goldie to work in the film industry, asked him to come to the set whenever he had time. Goldie would spend all his free time there doing odd jobs. He was not helping Chetan directly, but observed everything keenly. While watching Chetan direct a scene, he imagined how he would have done it differently. He saw how a particular shot looked on the screen and wondered about the many times the shot which looked impressive while being filmed did not look so in the editing room or on the screen. *Aandhiyan* did not impress the box office, but was selected for the Moscow Film Festival.

Uma didi asked Goldie to write a film script. Despite doubts, Goldie decided to give it a try, because of her faith in him.

He had also been reading the book, *20 Best Screenplays*. Goldie wrote during his commute to college. He would write even while sitting on the platform, waiting for his train. He showed his screenplay to Uma for her comments.

Chetan had worked in the All India Radio for a while and had become friends with sitar maestro Ravi Shankar and sarod maestro Ali Akbar Khan, who would visit his house frequently. Goldie spent a month with Ali Akbar Khan, learning music. Unbeknownst to him, he had picked up the nuances of Hindustani music and culture, which reflected in his writing as well.

Goldie finished writing his first screen play titled, *Taxi Driver.* He was not sure that the script would become a film, but he was sure that if that were to happen, it would be Dev Papa who would be the hero. He only wanted a heroine who would be a good match for his brother. The script was based on one Usman, a taxi driver who plied his taxi near their Pali Hill residence, and whose services they often used. Goldie believed that his script should reflect a common man's life. A taxi driver encounters different kinds of people in his life as customers. Uma believed, after reading the script, that it could be made into a movie. Navketan was not in a good shape financially. *Aandhiyan* and *Afsar* had bombed, and they needed a good script for the next movie. Uma showed Goldie's script to Dev.

Dev, busy with his career, had never taken Goldie's work seriously, though he knew the latter wrote and directed plays. Chetan would attend Goldie's plays once in a while and give suggestions. Once, when Goldie was not able to find an appropriate title for his play, Chetan suggested the title, *Gadbad*, after reading the script. The play was a super hit in college. But Dev had never watched any of Goldie's plays.

Dev agreed to hear Goldie's script; he would be interested in a particular script only if he liked the role he was envisaging for himself. (Goldie believed that Dev had little understanding of scripts). Dev liked the role of the taxi driver. The heroine could possibly be Kalpana Kartik, aka Mona Singha. Dev, after breaking up with Suraiya, had fallen for Kalpana, and was keen to produce the movie with Mona as the heroine. But all decisions regarding Navketan were being taken by Chetan. There was also the question of finding the right director. Keen that her husband should produce and direct a hit movie and make a name for himself, Uma suggested that Chetan should direct *Taxi Driver.*

Dev was sure that Chetan would not agree as he believed 'it was not his type'. But Chetan heard the script and agreed to go ahead. The budget was high as the script involved a lot of outdoor shooting. S.D. Burman was a family friend who had his music room in Navketan's studios. The songs were recorded, thus, in quick succession. After selecting the other actors for the film, Chetan started the shoot.

During the shooting, Dev called the Registrar of Marriages and got his marriage with Kalpana registered on the sets of the movie on 3 January, 1954.

Shot in 40 days, the film was ready for release after post-production work.

Busy studying, Goldie had not involved himself much in the shooting of the movie. He was just 19 years of age, and he saw the movie at the premiere show when it was released. He was happy to see his name under the 'story-screenplay' section. Navketan's manager Hamid, who was standing outside the theatre, congratulated him saying, 'Your hard work has borne fruit. The film is a hit.'

That was all! No one else really praised him. Till his death, he never got to hear such words. It was a case of familiarity breeding contempt. But it helped him to keep his head on his shoulders. Goldie did not take lack of praise to heart and focused on his college and plays. He had not thought about entering the film industry.

Goldie was now officially a part of Navketan Films as an assistant and earning a salary of ₹50 a month. He would manage his college fees and pocket money from what he earned. *Funtoosh* was being produced by Navketan then and Goldie would be on the sets after class. Goldie's job was to make copies of dialogues, do a little supervision, collect things, and help the actors rehearse their lines.

It was during the filming of *Funtoosh* that differences between Dev and Chetan began erupting. One day, it reached ugly proportions. The song, *Ae meri topi palat ke aa*, was being shot when Chetan left in a huff after arguing with Dev.

'Ask Goldie to shoot the scene,' he instructed while leaving.

Goldie thought it would be inappropriate to take over when his brother had left angrily. When he refused, Dev said, 'You take the shot. Chetan bhai has left.'

While Dev was in the makeup room, Goldie rushed to Chetan's house and asked why he had left so suddenly.

'Goldie, I am not upset. I am just not the kind of director Dev wants. I have to make these movies much against my wishes, using hero and heroines who run around trees singing songs, and with fights and other typical things that go into a commercial Hindi film. The kind of movies I want to make would not suit Dev. We set up Navketan so that all of us could work together and be successful. You understand Dev's personality better than I do, and will be able to direct the song better.'

Goldie returned to the set and directed the song. Chetan's assistant Prem Prakash assisted Goldie. The song was shot well – not only Dev, the audiences appreciated it too.

Chetan felt he was compromising himself making films with Dev. His own stories He wanted to focused more on the story than the hero and the heroine. But he was forced to make hero-oriented movies to suit Dev's style; Dev was also his partner. He decided it was time to leave Navketan to chase his own dreams. But not before training Goldie.

Uma did not want Goldie to pursue a film career. She believed this field corrupted character. She did not think the film industry the right place for a well-read, intelligent and cultured man. (In reality, Chetan was a highly-read intellectual). She voiced her views to Goldie once:

'This is not a field for intelligent people like you. I wish you won't enter this industry, but make a name for yourself elsewhere.'

Uma, who had encouraged Goldie to write the script for *Taxi Driver*, was in favour of him being a script writer though.

❖❖❖

Goldie was encouraged to write more scripts after the success of *Taxi Driver*. He wrote his next script without telling anyone. He also decided to take it elsewhere; he felt people thought

Chetan wrote the script for *Taxi Driver*, not he. Goldie was friendly with the staff at Navketan. The production manager, the business manager and everyone else, they all respected his views and suggestions. After a movie was made they would ask Goldie to give his views to Dev and Chetan.

Jovilal Parashar (J.L.), the general manager at Navketan, was who Goldie confided in about his new script.

The famous director, Shaheed Latif, was a family friend of the Anands. Dev had starred in his *Ziddi*. Latif's wife was the famous Urdu writer, Ismat Chughtai; he made films based on her stories. Around that time, Ismat had gone to China as part of a culture mission, and Latif was alone. Parashar knew Latif well and when they met, Latif said,

'I am looking for a good story.'

'Do you know Goldie wrote the story for *Taxi Driver*? He has written a script and I find that good. It would be apt for commercial cinema.'

'Goldie wrote the script? Isn't he still young and studying in college?'

'That is right. Why don't you read the script once?'

Latif agreed. Parashar asked Goldie to hand over the script to Parashar at his residence.

On the said day, Goldie reached Parashar's home. Goldie had the habit of writing a detailed script, with long shot, close-ups, mid-shot, action, scene 1, scene 2, outdoor, indoor, sunrise, sunset etc... He had a director's eye! He had learnt this from Chetan, whom he observed working at home. Chetan, realizing that Goldie was watching him write, would ask for his comments whenever he got stuck. Probably, he was encouraging Goldie to become a better scriptwriter!

Latif had seen Goldie since childhood and did not take him seriously. But he was surprised when Goldie read out the script, with its immaculate details. Latif was so impressed with the script that he offered Goldie a cheque of ₹500 on the spot.

'This is just a signing amount. I will pay you ₹5000 once we start shooting,' Latif added.

It was Goldie's first earning – he had not received a single rupee for *Taxi Driver.*

Goldie was in seventh heaven as he left Latif's house, but the elation did not last long. Ismat returned from China and was upset when told that Latif had taken Goldie's script.

'What about me if you start taking scripts from outside? You cannot take stories from anyone else.'

This led to a lot of arguments, with Latif finally deciding not to take Goldie's script.

Goldie was unaware of the arguments and assumed that the film would be shot soon. Told by Parashar that the film had been delayed, he continued to hope even though nothing happened as months went by.

When he enquired with Parashar, he came to know the real issue and was terrible disappointed. He wondered whom he could approach. Around that time producer Nyaya Sharma had finished shooting *Kinare Kinare,* starring Dev and Meena Kumari, and directed by Chetan. Sharma came to know of Goldie's script and approached him, saying,

'I am told you had taken a script to Shaheed Latif. Why don't you read that out to me?'

'I need to take Latif sir's permission. He has given me a signing amount, so it is his first right.'

Goldie asked Latif if it was fine for him to take back his script and return the signing amount.

'Dear, you can take the script and keep the signing amount as well,' Latif assured Goldie.

Goldie read the script to Nyayaa and his team. They all liked what they heard. Nyaya took out ₹500 from his pocket, saying he would produce the film. Goldie had got a signing amount of a ₹1000 for the script!

Nyaya discussed the script with Goldie often, but things on the financial front were not coming together.

Goldie had bought a suit and new clothes for himself, using the signing amount. He had not told anyone at home, but

Parashar had informed Chetan and Dev of the deal. But they did not quiz Goldie about it. Goldie, too, felt that he was grown up now and could take decisions independently. He wanted to establish his own identity and not be known as Dev Anand's and Chetan Anand's brother. His writing and directing plays in college had given him the confidence to direct a movie if given an opportunity. Uma was keen to send him to the US for higher studies. Goldie loved to paint and was impressed by Walt Disney's cartoons, so she was keen that he should go west and pursue his passion. In the meanwhile, Goldie completed his graduation and enrolled for M.A.

Nyaya was busy casting the actors for the movie. His director, though, was not sure of Goldie's script. The director had suggested some changes in the script that Goldie was not particularly in favour of. After a few meetings, Goldie told the director,

'If you keep changing the script, the very essence of the story will fail. Better to not make the movie on my script.'

Goldie's pride was the result of Chetan's influence who had told Goldie often that the only person who could change the script was the script writer himself. He had told Goldie that it was better not to go ahead with the script than make changes to it.

❖❖❖

Goldie concluded that it wasn't necessary to decide on the script yet. Around the same time, Chetan, too, decided to leave Navketan Films and make *Joru Ka Bhai* on his own. Chetan was aware of Goldie's inclination towards acting and chose to cast him in his film being produced under the banner of Himalaya Films. The film, a comedy, was Goldie's first appearance on the silver screen. The film also starred Balraj Sahni, Johnny Walker and Sheila Ramani, but didn't fare too well at the box office.

In the meantime, Goldie got to know that Dev had signed Raj Khosla to direct Navketan's *Khali Botal.* Dev had given the reins of direction of Navketan films to Khosla after Chetan left. *Khali Botal* was written by Rajinder Singh Bedi and nothing other than the title was ready. Goldie was sure that once Khosla decided on the story, he would start having doubts about it, and then look for a new story. The same pattern would continue and Khosla would remain undecided till the end. Once eight or nine reels of a film were shot, his doubts would keep growing and he would end up choosing a new story every few months. But this wasn't acceptable at Navketan. They had a tradition of making one film a year. They had all their staff, in production, publicity and technical, departments, on a monthly pay. Moreover, Navketan wasn't profitable enough to afford salaries for two years without making a film. Even after eight months Khosla was undecided on a story. Everything was uncertain.

It wouldn't be an exaggeration to say that Parashar contributed to Goldie's film career in a big way. He loved Goldie and, owing to that love and the respect he had for Goldie's talent and abilities, he wanted Goldie to succeed. Parashar spoke to every contact of his. Realizing that Khosla was taking too much time deciding on a story and that Goldie's script was ready, Parashar went to Dev and said, 'Goldie has a script that he had given to Shaheed Latif. But Ismat Chughtai did not allow that. Nyaya Sharma had taken the script and also paid Goldie some money for it. I am not sure whether Nyaya Sharma will use the script. But I am certain that this script will be a hit. I feel we must have a look at it. Raj Khosla is still stuck with story selection and if you like the script, you can make the film with some other director.'

Since Goldie's *Taxi Driver* had been a success, Dev decided to give the script a shot.

'Alright, tell Goldie to narrate the script to me.'

Although the affection between Dev and Goldie hadn't reduced with age, communication between them had reduced unintentionally over the years. Parashar passed Dev's message to Goldie, who responded saying, 'You please tell Dev bhai that

I will narrate the script only on the condition that I will direct the film myself.' Parashar promptly passed on Goldie's message to Dev.

'Idiot… is he mad or what? His education isn't over yet – and does he even know what direction is all about? Subodh Mukherjee and Nasir Hussain have worked so hard to become directors. Goldie hasn't even worked as an assistant director for one full film, and he wants to be a director? Is that even possible? Tell him to drop this stupidity and narrate the script.'

Dev was annoyed by Goldie's decision on direction and Parashar went back to Goldie with his message. But Goldie stuck to his demand.

Dev rejected the proposal yet again. 'This is not possible. What film will Goldie make? We need a story that Raj can direct.' Dev almost dropped the idea of Goldie's script.

'This is not a script suitable for Raj Khosla's style. The way I have written the story, only Latif saheb or I can make it. Latif saheb has made moves like *Ziddi* and knows how to project Dev Anand on the screen. Since he is unable to direct it at present, I will direct it myself.' Goldie stuck to his stance and so did Dev.

Two months went by and the Navketan staff had to be paid their salaries. Khosla hadn't zeroed in on a story yet and shooting looked like a distant dream. All the staff sat idle and one day the Navketan cameraman, Virendra Ratra, requested Dev to speak to Goldie.

Ratra was very highly regarded in the Anand family and his opinions were taken seriously. Finally, Dev agreed to listen to Goldie's story narration. Dev loved going to Mahabaleshwar on weekends. He asked Virendra to tell Goldie to come to Mahabaleshwar with the script.

Goldie excitedly agreed. The same day, Goldie, Dev, Kalpana Kartik and Virendra drove to Mahabaleshwar. Goldie had hidden his script under his shirt as if it was something priceless.

'I heard you have written a script,' Dev said casually.

'Yes.'

'Okay, let's hear it.'

Goldie began reading his script. The script was written with the minutest detail in mind and proved that the script writer had a deep understanding of the filmmaking process. This was not a script written only for the writer, but also for the director.

Goldie completed his reading, but Dev Anand didn't react at all. The moment they reached their usual place of stay, Hotel Fredrick, Dev booked a trunk call on the hotel telephone. It was to his production manager, Thakkar.

'Thakkar, book Kardar Studios for ten days. Production number eight has been postponed for some reason. We are starting production number nine and Goldie will be directing it.'

That film was *Nau Do Gyarah.*

Dev, Goldie and the rest returned to Mumbai after two days, and preparations for the film began in earnest. The first item on the list was the music. Sachin Dev Burman was Navketan's favourite music composer – it was sure he would compose the music for the film. Goldie had his own ideas about how the songs should be. Most songs in Hindi films were there only as fillers and had nothing to do with the story. Goldie made it clear to S.D. Burman about the kind of songs he wanted for the film.

'Dada, the songs of the movie should be as if the hero and heroine are having a conversation. I don't want songs with heavy words, or the words the heroine croons with flowers falling from a tree, or the typical situation where the hero is sing on a running horse carriage. These are very common. The songs I am looking for should be a part of the storyline, and if they are removed the story would be affected.'

Goldie believed that if the presence or absence of a song made no difference, why have them in the first place? Burman da and lyricist Majrooh Sultanpuri got down to creating the songs. The tune for the song, *Aajaa panchhi akela hai,* was suggested by Sachin da's wife, Meera. Majrooh wrote *sunehra baadal* as the second line for the song *Aankhon mein kya ji.*

Goldie told Majrooh, 'Why not make it *rupahala baadal* instead? I am going to shoot the song in moonlight, so *sunehra* won't be suitable.'

Majrooh was impressed by Goldie's understanding and intelligence.

S.D. Burman encouraged Goldie, giving the 22-year-old a lot of confidence.

During the same time, Dev was working in a film by Subodh Mukherjee. Goldie had heard that if there was a foreign movie running in either Eros, Strand or Regal theatres, Mukherjee would ask his writer-director to watch the movie and incorporate good scenes from that movie into his own. Mukherjee had three or four writers working on the same film at a time. Other directors, too, would pick up content from foreign films and Indianise them to suit local tastes. The film industry was small and there were very few editors. The big stars worked in ten films at the same time and character actors in fifteen films simultaneously. The actors would note the scenes their director-producer had taken from a foreign film and tell this to the other filmmakers they worked with, and induce them to do the same. There were no cinema academies and acting schools then and even the established stars of the time would watch their favourite foreign film star's movies multiple times.

For instance, Dilip Kumar had made Marlon Brando his role model and loved watching Brando's films. He had told Goldie that he would take the morning train from Malad's Bombay Talkies all the way to Churchgate and watch the same film repeatedly for three days, and yet he never understood how the foreign actors acted so well. He felt Indian stars were too loud. Dilip Kumar was deeply influenced by Marlon Brando, while Dev emulated Gregory Peck and watched all of Gregory's films without fail. Such things were not hidden at that time. The Indian film stars copying their foreign role models and the

Indian directors copying and getting inspired by scenes from foreign films was a common practice and wasn't frowned upon. Dev, too, felt that Goldie should watch a few foreign films and get inspired, but Goldie was of the opinion that filmmaking is an art. It is like a complete diagram and cannot be made with pieces taken from here and there. He said, 'If the film I am making is not mine, then it is nobody's'. That was why Goldie swore that he would not watch any foreign film till his own film was complete.

Dev asked Goldie before he began shooting, 'Which scene are you shooting first?'

'The climax.'

'You are being childish! Don't be stubborn. All great directors complete the film first. Discuss with people and then shoot the climax.'

'Maybe, but I have written this climax and irrespective of its length, my climax will not change. Whether I shoot my script from the beginning or the end, nothing is going to change. I will not change a word of my script. You don't worry.'

A few scenes with actress Lalita Pawar were to be shot on the first day. Lalita called Goldie immediately after the first shot and said, 'This is the first time I am working with a director after V. Shantaram. There are very few directors like him.'

Goldie could not understand what Lalita meant at that time. Goldie felt that V. Shantaram made his actors over-act, but he respected Shantaram's technical brilliance. Shantaram had carved a niche for himself in the Indian film industry, and had built his own studio. Goldie had immense respect for Shantaram, and so found her words intriguing. He belonged to the 'natural school' of filmmaking, but once his creativity began to be appreciated, he truly understood what she had meant.

After that Goldie went to Delhi with his unit and shot parts of the film on the Delhi-Mumbai highway. The whole unit stayed at the PWD guest-house during the shoot.

Goldie was shooting the song, *Hum hain rahi pyaar ke,* on the highway. When the second para of the song was being shot, there was some technical glitch and the machine stopped working. Nobody had a clue whether they would be able to set the machine right or how long it would take. But Goldie refused to cancel the shoot. He knew the words of the song by heart and he shot the rest of the song on the beat with himself singing the song.

There were no modern sound systems those days and the dialogues were said without the soundtrack. Also, there were no tape recorders or sound recorders – they had to know Dev's dialogues in every scene for the dubbing.

After shooting about six reels of the film, some indoor scenes were shot at the Kardar Studios in Mumbai. Goldie then went to Mahabaleshwar with his unit to shoot some outdoor scenes.

Character actor Jeevan, who acted in *Nau Do Gyarah,* wrote a letter to Goldie on the last day of his shoot. 'I have never seen a director like you. I will be ready to work with you anytime you want.'

Goldie's confidence rose with the positive feedback he received from Jeevan and Lalita Pawar.

There was a lot of authenticity in the shooting and that was the specialty of this film. A girl runs away from home and meets a boy... this had rarely been seen on screen before. Goldie kept telling his production manager during the shooting that he was making a hit film. That was the kind of confidence he had.

Goldie didn't regret the fact that he never worked as an assistant director with anyone; had he done that, he believed, he would never have been able to do what he was doing. His direction was not influenced by any director. Since he had no formal training, Goldie experimented a lot with his work.

Goldie would often tell Ratra where the camera should be placed.

'But the trolley will not move there. The set is coming in the way,' the cameraman would say.

'I want the trolley to be there,' Goldie would insist, and tell the art director that he wanted the camera to go through the set door.

'But that is not possible.'

'Then break this door and make a new one. My trolley has to go through the door.'

Goldie was a hot-blooded young man maturing with age. The shooting was over in nine months.

The editing continued for thirteen continuous days at Famous Studios, Tardeo. The studio had been destroyed in a fire, but there was an editing room at the back that Goldie used. He even slept there, not leaving for eleven days at a stretch. It was his nature to plunge into work relentlessly.

The film not only made Goldie a director, but also taught him the art of editing.

Dev had asked Dharamveer, an editor of repute, to assist Goldie in the making of *Nau Do Gyarah,* realizing that Goldie's experience in direction was little. Dharamveer was a regular editor for most of Dev's films.

Goldie, a natural learner, keenly observed how the films were edited. Luckily, Goldie's directorial style lent itself to little editing.

Differences erupted between Dharamveer and Goldie while editing the climax. Normally, most films had the hero and the villain fighting, chasing each other in fast cars, shooting with guns etc. The film used to end with the hero winning. Goldie wanted something different to engage the viewer. He showed the villain challenging the hero by saying, 'If you don't do this in five minutes, I will kill the heroine.'

Goldie was reading *Yoga Vasistha* those days, in which time is shown as subjective. A night of sorrow is long for a woman, but passes in a blink during a honeymoon. Speed of time, hence, was subject to a man's mental state. Goldie wanted the five minutes to look like five hours for the viewer. Each character glances at their respective wrist watches every now and then. Goldie showed the image of the watch every ten seconds.

In a novel we read of different scenes being enacted at the same time. Goldie used the same treatment for his climax. He showed what different people were experiencing in those five minutes. The scene stretched to nearly eight minutes instead of five. Dharamveer berated Goldie gently in Punjabi saying,

'*Goldie ji, aisa nahin honda. Log uth jayenge, cigarette pe chale jayenge...*' He wanted to edit the scene.

Dharamveer feared that the viewer would not tolerate a long climax and would walk out. But Goldie was adamant. Dharamveer told Dev before sending the film to sound-recordist, B.N. Sharma,

'You please make him understand.'

Dev agreed with Dharamveer, deciding to talk to Goldie. But Goldie was in no mood to listen.

Even Sharma, who was well respected for his craft, agreed that the scene was a tad too long. Likewise, many others, too, were in favour of editing the scene.

Goldie realized that there may be some element of truth with so many people advising against the length, but his heart was not willing to accept the suggestion. He believed in his instinct.

The sound-recordist ensured that the music changed each second to match the movement of the clock. The overall effect was good, but Goldie realized that the viewer may be looking for more. He said,

'Let us take this version for the premier. We will see the reaction. Else, we will show the edited version in the next show.'

Goldie did not show any enthusiasm once the film was ready. In fact, he did not even attend the premiere and was in college.

He reached the theatre after the first show to find Ahmed Jaffery, the production manager of Navketan, and Parashar there. They congratulated him, 'You are finally a director!'

The viewers had enjoyed the film, especially the climax.

Goldie then travelled along with the film to various

theatres, watching viewer response to the climax scene. He could see people screaming, sitting on the edge of their seats. The sound of whistles told him that people loved the scene.

Goldie realized that he would not have succeeded had he listened to the editor.

A film, made on a moderate budget of just ₹5 lakhs had become a hit.

The film paved the way for Dev's light comedies in the future, with songs taking the story forward. Goldie had become famous with his very first movie. Chetan's exit made it difficult for Navketan to remain successful with Dev busy with outside projects at the same time. But Goldie's success strengthened Navketan. His talent assured Dev he was not alone.

While directing *Nau Do Gyarah,* Goldie was signed as a lead actor in *Agra Road.* He had acted in plays and used to read books on the subject. He would read aloud dialogues from Shakespeare sitting at the seashore, improvising on his dialogue delivery to make them more effective.

Everyone believed that Goldie, being Dev's younger brother, would become an actor one day. His principal at Poddar School definitely believed so. Goldie, influenced by Chetan who he felt was the wisest of the lot, did think an actor's job was dependent on others, but took up the role in *Agra Road* to fulfil his desire to act.

Ravindra Dave, was more of a traditionalist director, and Goldie, with his understated style, was not very comfortable. He had to obey the director's command. His stint as an actor did not help Goldie much. He realized he could not act under someone else's direction.

The success of *Nau Do Gyarah* had not gone to Goldie's head. Happy to have proved himself, he now planned to finish his M.A. studies.

Raj Khosla was busy directing *Khali Botal,* which was renamed *Kala Pani.* Navketan produced only one movie at a time, so the next film had to wait anyway.

Khosla suffered a personal tragedy with the death of his

son while *Kala Pani* was being completed. It shattered him, and he was often seen crying in Navketan's office. Dev put the responsibility of post-production, recording etc on Goldie. But Goldie suffered from a kidney problem around the same time and was admitted to Nanavati Hospital.

This was in 1958, a year and a month after the release of *Nau Do Gyarah*. Dev was on a trip to Russia. Chetan was scared when the doctor said,

'There is water retention in the kidney. An urgent operation is needed to avoid complications.' The operation, done by a Dr. Joshi, went on for three hours. Goldie was left very weak, and his recovery took about eight months. He turned religious after the incident, believing a miracle had saved him. He had barely recovered when the problem resurfaced. The unbearable pain made him want to kill himself. Morphine left him dull and he often lay listlessly on his bed. When he got better, he took off for Ooty to recuperate.

❖❖❖

Goldie incorporated real-life events into his script for *Kala Bazar*. The character of the college student was somewhat based on his own experiences. Buying movie tickets in the black market, or seeing others do so, helped him to develop the character of the heroine. The heroine is so against the whole idea of the black market that she tears the tickets her lover has bought in black. The hero sees two characters: a boy who does not mind the black market and the heroine who cannot tolerate it at all. The morals and values of the heroine give the hero a shock, changing his life.

It was assumed that Dev would play the hero in the film. The pair of Dev Anand and Waheeda Rehman in *Solva Saal, C.I.D.* etc. had been a big hit, and she was selected for the lead female role. The role of the heroine's sister was not big but Nanda, who had played similar roles, was chosen for the same.

The philosophical angle of the movie was inspired by

Goldie's own experiences. While recuperating from his illness, he had visited Ooty and stayed in a film distributor's house in Bangalore. He met a religious guru there, who influenced Goldie so much that he became his disciple. Later, after returning to Bombay, Goldie would get up at 2 a.m., bathe, and sit down to pray to Lord Shiva. He even turned vegetarian.

Goldie read Swami Vivekananda's books, the Upanishads, the Gita and other religious and philosophical texts. He was also influenced by books on the Buddha. He wanted to travel barefoot, with a *kamandalu* in hand, from Kanyakumari to the Himalayas, like an ascetic. Inspired by his dreams, he bestowed a philosophical angle to the hero in *Kala Bazar* – the hero repents his sins. Goldie wanted to convey the message that remorse was the real punishment. Physical punishment is unnecessary if a man truly experiences remorse. This was the theme of *Kala Bazar*. Goldie had the example of Valmiki, a dacoit who turned into a writer and wrote the *Ramayana* read by millions. Goldie believed everyone should get a chance to repent and transform themselves.

Goldie had incorporated an American judgement into the script. The accused had done something that helped people, but was a crime in the eyes of the law. The people were in his support – the judge, too, at a personal level believed that he should not be punished. But in keeping with the spirit of the law, the judge pronounced one day of imprisonment which ended when the court ended. Goldie was impressed reading about it in the newspaper and decided to end his movie in a similar manner.

Due to certain circumstances, the hero in *Kala Bazar* was forced into black marketing. He leaves his trade to earn an honest income, asking others, too, to do so. He returns the ₹5000 he had stolen from a lawyer, telling him he had a right to take him to the police. But the lawyer is impressed by his earnest effort to become a good man and does not report him.

Later, the hero is caught by the police. The same lawyer defends him in court. Arguing in favour of the hero, the lawyer appeals that putting such a man in jail to 'correct' him is unfair as he has already started walking that path. Not just that, he has transformed his friends, too. The judge is convinced and lets the hero go with one day's punishment for the crime. The day ends as the court ends. The movie finishes with this scene.

The government lawyer, Kishore Sahu, and the hero's lawyer, Chetan Anand, enact the last scene beautifully.

But the movie got stuck at the Censor Board as the board wanted the criminal to be shown as being punished. Goldie tried his level best to explain, but to no avail. The Censor Board chief declined to hear his pleas.

The movie was criticized even in the Parliament on how people are taught black marketing.

Goldie had no option but to change the last scene. When the hero and his friends are sent to jail, the friends complain that there was no point in good behaviour as they would once again turn to illegal means when they are released. The hero appeals to his friends by threatening to fast unto death until they promise to change themselves. Goldie had to cut both the court scene and the last scene to fit the length, but it left him disappointed and dissatisfied.

Goldie was upset at the Censor Board. He always regretted the fact that despite India being a democratic country, he was never able to show what he really wanted to. He firmly believed that the board should e an independent body and not under the government. He did not believe in censorship. A city could tolerate a hundred thousand prostitutes who even a 14-year-old boy could visit, but the Censor Board had the powers to decide whether a movie should be screened or not. He felt that the board could have given a certification stating 'not for children below 18.' Goldie did not believe that cinema changed people's minds. If that was the case, lovers would be dancing around trees singing songs!

Goldie's anger was against the members of the Censor Board who insulted and spoke arrogantly to film directors and producers. They behaved like school headmasters berating a truant child. They thought filmmakers were spoiling the moral fabric of society and that it was their duty to save the society from such rot.

Goldie saw the board members as blinkered, narrow-minded people who had no right to advise filmmakers.

Kala Bazar turned out to be a big hit. Songs like *Khoya khoya chand, Apni toh har aah, Sache huye sapne, Rimjhim ke taraane* are popular even today.

It was when Burman da was composing music for *Khoya khoya chand....*

Goldie, explaining the situation to Burman da:

'Dada, it is a full-moon night in Ooty and there is silence everywhere. In the distance are the tea gardens. The hero realizes that the heroine likes him and is running around the town, happy and carefree. The song needs openness and a high pitch.'

Burman nodded and fiddled with his harmonium.

But the next moment he started snapping his fingers and instructed his assistant, Maruti, 'Get the rhythm.'

Burman da then stood up and started humming. He said, after a few moments, 'Yes! Wow! Yes, yes, wait a moment.... I am getting it.' Lyricist Shailendra was present. He lit a cigarette and said, 'I will be back in a moment.'

He returned shortly in the silent night and said,

'Dada, listen to this... these are dummy words... *khoya khoya chaand, khula aasmaan*.' The words fitted the tune so well that Goldie said,

'Burman da, the song is ready. Let the words be. But the antara should end on a high note.'

Burman da was excited and started working and Shailendra promised to return the next day with the entire song. The next day when Shailendra got the entire song and asked Goldie to select the length, he was confused – all the stanzas were good!

Kala Bazar premiered in the Royal Opera House, Bombay, in January 1960. Goldie firmly believed that had the Censor

Board not asked the climax scene to be changed, the film would have done even better.

He had directed *Nau Do Gyarah* to prove himself, but he stepped into the world of cinema with *Kala Bazar.* He started getting offers from other countries, but Goldie would do nothing. He used to take long breaks between movies, sometimes falling ill.

❖❖❖

Navketan's publicity manager Amarjeet, who used to earlier assist Chetan in film direction, helped Goldie too. Amarjeet had also been with Goldie through his post-operative period and accompanied to Ooty and Bangalore. They had become close friends, and Goldie never considered him an employee or assistant.

Goldie wanted to sponsor him to study a course in publicity in the US, but Amarjeet was keen on becoming a director. He requested Goldie to give him a chance; they had discussed this in Ooty. While returning from Ooty, they stayed at a film distributor's house in Bangalore. This was where Goldie came to know of a famous astrologer and decided to visit him.

Apart from philosophy, Goldie was also interested in palmistry, *kundali,* astrology and allied subjects. Despite a long queue at the astrologer's place, Goldie was ushered in quickly, thanks to the distributor's influence. The elderly astrologer sat like a *munim,* an accountant from an older era, leaning against fat bolsters, with a small wooden table in front of him. Clients had to write three questions on a piece of paper and hand it to him with ₹5. Without reading the paper, the old man would open a book and read from it in Sanskrit, the only language he knew. That would answer the questions just asked.

Both Amarjeet and Goldie wrote their respective questions and gave the chits to the astrologer.

The astrologer, reading the answer to Amarjeet's first question, said in Sanskrit, 'The one sitting on your right!'

Amarjeet had asked the name of the person who would

help him fulfil his ambition and was a true friend. Goldie took this as a divine sign that he must help Amarjeet direct a film.

One of Goldie's questions was regarding Raj Kumar Anand, a family member in prison for murder. Despite the whole family trying, they had not been able to get him out on bail. Goldie's question was about Raj Kumar's release. Raj Kumar should not talk to two friends who may betray him, was the advice he got. The astrologer gave a date on which Raj Kumar would be released and said that a friend whose name began with K would betray Raj Kumar and spill the beans to the police.

Things played out exactly the way the astrologer had predicted. The police managed to convince Raj Kumar's friend to turn witness. Goldie returned to Mumbai and tried to convince Raj Kumar's friends not to give false statements against him.

There were many stories about the murder accusation. One was that while working in the police department, he had beating a man to death. Another was that Raj Kumar had beaten the physically abusive husband of the woman he loved and that he later died. But these were only stories.

Raj Kumar had gone to watch a movie with a friend and his wife. Raj Kumar then dropped the couple at their home in Bandra, where a drunk man made some crude comments about the friend's wife. When the drunk man got violent, Raj Kumar hit him with a stick. The man fell and died a few hours later. Raj Kumar had not intended to kill him, and the man had not died instantly.

Raj Kumar was accused of manslaughter by a woman who had apparently witnessed the scene. 'I heard his screams and came out of my hut to see Raj Kumar hitting him,' she told the judge. Goldie was of the opinion that the police were looking for a bribe; since Raj Kumar belonged to the film fraternity, they thought him rich. In reality, Raj Kumar was yet to make his mark in the industry and could hardly be called rich. The police were trying to find false witnesses to pin him down.

During cross-examination, Raj Kumar's lawyer was able to show that the woman had not really seen anything to be able to give a true statement. The jury set Raj Kumar free.

The experiences in prison had turned Raj Kuma bitter. A once genial man, he was now filled with negative thoughts. Except for a few family members and a couple of friends, all others had turned their back on him. The film industry had literally shunned him. Producers not only did not make him any new offers, but also cancelled earlier contracts.

Goldie decided to help Amarjeet. He started thinking of a story for him when in Bangalore. He had often wanted to write a story on untouchables; he wrote a love story on the rebirth of a Brahmin girl and a Harijan youth. As the society does not allow them to come together, they decide to meet in their next birth. This time he is born a Brahmin, while she is born in a low-caste household. Once again, the society rejects them. Realizing that Dev Papa may not suit the role, Goldie decided to act himself. He had a hidden desire to act! His role in *Kala Bazar,* though small, had been praised. He had received a few offers but, being busy, had not considered them. Now that Amarjeet was to direct a movie, he cast himself in the lead role. He thought of Nutan for the heroine's role. Amarjeet liked the script and they both decided to meet Dev in Bombay.

Dev heard the script and promptly rejected it. Goldie knew why: it was not possible to make any film in Navketan that did not star Dev. But Goldie persisted.

'If we can make *Kala Pani* without me, then why not a film without you? We will start two movies at the same time. You work in one and I in the other.'

Dev was upset, but did not say anything for a while. He was against Goldie acting in a film and criticized the script as being outdated.

Dev was also not in favour of Amarjeet as the director, but Goldie said he had given his word to Amarjeet.

'Then look for another story,' Dev said.

Many people came to Navketan, looking for work. One of them was Sarkar, who narrated a story of two similar looking men who were in the army. It was a small episode that he narrated, based on World War II. Goldie liked the outline and decided to write a script on it.

'You must direct this movie,' Dev told Goldie.

'I have given my word to Amarjeet. He will be the director.'

Dev realized that Goldie was determined, and agreed on the condition that Goldie should take all the responsibility, and that if anything were to go wrong, he would step in. Goldie readily agreed.

Goldie went to Kashmir in a jeep, taking along with him his friend, Satyadev Dubey, Dev's driver Brij Mohan, and Amarjeet. He would write whenever they halted at some place, be it a dak bungalow or a hotel. In Kashmir, they hired a houseboat. In those twenty days, Goldie finished working on the script. On returning to Bombay, he read it out to Dev, who was suitably impressed and ordered the shoot to begin.

Goldie was not just the scriptwriter for the film, but played an important part in its music too. Jaidev had come in as Ustad Ali Akbar Khan's assistant, and had become S.D. Burman's assistant once Ali Akbar Khan left Navketan. Goldie wanted to give Jaidev a chance and *Hum Dono* became the perfect vehicle. Apparently, those days Lata Mangeshkar was not on talking terms with Jaidev and had boycotted him, but Dev managed to convince Lata so that she agreed to lend her voice to the songs. Jaidev wanted *Allah tero naam* to be sung by M.S. Subbulakshmi, but Lata did not agree, insisting on singing both the bhajans in the movie. Dev agreed, and Lata sang the other bhajan *Prabhu tero naam*, too.

Sadhana and Nanda were cast as the two heroines. Sadhana had made her debut with the hit film, *Love in Simla*, and Nanda was a friend. Goldie believed Nanda was as talented as Meena Kumari, and wanted to give her the lead role. She had been upset playing a sister in *Kala Bazar*.

The dialogues of *Hum Dono* were the film's high point.

One could say the movie was, in fact, dialogue-based. Goldie was normally against too many dialogues as he wanted the acting to speak, but knowing that Amarjeet may not be comfortable with that approach, he stressed on dialogue this time. It would make the job of the actors that much easier.

The shooting began. Amarjeet did not have the skills of a director, but Goldie did not want to teach him or guide him on the set in the presence of everyone. He would elaborate on each scene, including camera setting and its arrangement, at home the previous day before the shot began. He would even draw sketches for Amarjeet's understanding. Amarjeet often found it difficult to follow Goldie's instructions and would instruct the camera to roll in the opposite direction, leading to arguments with the cameraman. It happened the very first day of the shoot. Apparently, Amarjeet was holding the sketch wrongly. This continued for a few days – each time Amarjeet making the same mistake. Goldie thought it best to leave Amarjeet on his own. He believed he would learn to swim if thrown into the deep end. Unfortunately, Goldie's assumption turned out wrong. When he saw the rushes, a lot of film had to be thrown away.

Dev wanted to fire Amarjeet, but Goldie intervened.

Sadhana would consult Goldie before a shot as she was new to films. Goldie would sit in a corner, discreetly giving instructions to Amarjeet, so no one realized that Amarjeet was not directing the movie.

On 19 October, 1930, a scene was being shot in Mehboob Studio for *Hum Dono*: Sadhana takes her lover (Dev) home to meet her father (Gajanan Jagirdar). In the script, Goldie had shown the hero awestruck by the heroine's palatial bungalow, realizing he was unlikely to be accepted by her father. He feels 'small', and does not want to step into the house, but he doesn't have a choice as he has been invited. In the script, Sadhana holds a hesitant Dev's hand and leads him into the house. Dev said, after reading the scene, 'I will go in myself. I don't need to be led.'

'That is because you are not Dev Anand here. You are an ordinary man in love with a very rich girl. Your pride does not allow you to enter her house. Her love drags you into the house, but you leave the place seeing its splendour. You suffer from an inferiority complex,' Goldie tried explaining.

In the scene the heroine's father tells the hero that he would never be able to provide such luxury to his daughter – ever! He insults him though he was telling the truth. Snubbed, the hero decides to join the army. It was, thus, a very crucial scene.

'But I should not be led like a dog,' Dev insisted.

Goldie gave up then, saying he was not the director. He didn't like the way Dev Papa had snubbed him on the sets. He stepped back and sat in the shadows though no one realized he was sulking. Upset with Dev, he stepped out of the studio and sat at the Bombay Lodge restaurant on Warden Road. Sipping coffee, he sat there for almost three hours, trying to compose himself.

'I will never go to the sets of *Hum Dono*. Let them make the film the way they want to,' Goldie fumed, when his driver Brij Mohan came searching for him. Realizing that Goldie had been hurt, it was Dev who sent Brij Mohan to search for Goldie at his favourite joint.

'Dev sahab has said that he would not shoot without your presence.'

Goldie returned to Mehboob Studio as he did not want the shooting to be interrupted. He returned and started working as if nothing had happened!

The shot was arranged and Sadhana, holding Dev's hand, leads him into the house. Amarjeet and everyone around realized that Dev would not shoot without Goldie. With the reins actually held by Goldie, Amarjeet got a shot at being a director. Despite directing the whole movie, Goldie stuck to his word and allowed the direction to be credited to Amarjeet.

Hum Dono got accolades from the viewers, no doubt, but it was Dev who was truly impressed by Goldie's work. During the shooting, Goldie had told Dev that he was playing a double role – that of an army major, Vijay Verma, and the other one where Dev could be himself. Viewers loved both Dev Anands. What they did not know was that it was Goldie who stood as one Dev Anand when the shot required both Dev Anands to be filmed together.

An incident that took place while the movie was being shot shook Goldie to the core. Uma decided to separate from Chetan and left the house one day. She wanted to marry Ebrahim Alkazi, who headed the National School of Drama. She knew Goldie would not allow her to leave home, and so she lied to him, saying she was visiting her parents. Goldie was so upset when he came to know the truth that he decided never to speak to her again.

Hum Dono was the official entry for the Berlin International Film Festival. In 1962, six films were selected for the festivals in Berlin, Melbourne, Sydney, Czechoslovakia, etc. on recommendations of the Film Federation of India.

Dev wanted Goldie to accompany him to Berlin, but Goldie felt that he would get neglected there. The festival attracted people from all creative fields. He was not the official director though he was the scriptwriter. Goldie suggested that he could introduce the film there, as 'Vijay Anand presents Dev Anand', but Dev did not like the suggestion.

On Dev's request, Goldie finally agreed to attend the festival. He saw Amarjeet's true colours there when the latter showed him a set of cards that said Vijay Anand was 'writer', while his own cards said, 'director'.

Amarjeet knew that Goldie was impressive enough, and in order to prevent people from assuming that he was the director, Amarjeet had printed the cards stating Goldie as the writer. Goldie had made Amarjeet the director, but clearly his friend did not feel any gratitude. It was only for Amarjeet that he had taken a backseat. Clearly, not only had Amarjeet forgotten the favour, he was suffering from an inferiority complex.

Despite being upset, Goldie enjoyed the festival, meeting greats like James Stuart and Shirley MacLaine among others.

Hum Dono received the kind of praise that no other movie in the festival got. But Dev and Goldie also had to face some critics. There was an allegation that *Hum Dono* had been copied from the English film, *Libel*. Dev clarified that the story was based on a real incident during World War II and that it was up to the critics to decide whether to believe them or not.

After returning from Berlin, Amarjeet continued to put Goldie down in various conversations. But Goldie chose to ignore the rant of an insecure person. He did not believe in getting into arguments. Hence, when Amarjeet called Goldie for the setting of a song in *Teen Devian,* Goldie presented himself. S.D. Burman, while respecting Dev, would always take Goldie's advice when it came to songs.

Goldie never tried to take the credit for the success of *Hum Dono*. But when people started comparing Amarjeet's *Teen Devian* and *Gambler* to *Hum Dono*, Goldie had to clarify and tell the truth. He knew that telling the truth would not spoil Amarjeet's career as a director.

Little did Goldie know then that he would have similar experiences with Nasir Hussain and Gulshan Rai.

❖❖❖

Cameraman Jal Mistry had good relations with Dev and Goldie, and when he decided to produce a movie, they both offered to help. He entrusted Goldie with the task of direction, with Tolaram Jalan of Filmistan Studios as financier. The lead actors for the proposed film, *Kahin Aur Chal,* were Dev Anand and Asha Parekh – pairing them up again after *Hum Dono*. The story centered around an extra-marital affair. The hero comes to know of his wife's affair, but he is unable to confront her or her lover. In a fit of rage, he shoots the lover one day, and then runs away to escape being caught. Tired of running, he tries to commit suicide but the heroine (Asha Parekh) and her friends save his life. Soon the heroine falls in love with him, but he is unable to reveal his past. He takes on a new name and a job, and whenever exposed, runs away to try his luck elsewhere.

One day, he sees someone who resembles the person he had shot – the person had never died! He wonders if he had wasted his entire life running from the police.

The story was short and succinct. If the film is heavily dependent on the story, the role of the director is reduced considerably. Goldie believed that a film should rely on the director's inputs rather than the storyline for its success. *Jewel Thief* and *Teesri Manzil* do not look outdated even today. Goldie liked stories where the director made a lot of difference and the script evolved accordingly. In his opinion, the script should tell only part of the story.

The music was by Shankar-Jaikishan, as suggested by Jal Mistry. The duo was at the top of the music industry, and Goldie enjoyed working with them. Both Shankar and Jaikishan were very disciplined and punctual. They would discuss the songs in the first meeting and be ready with the tunes when they met again. They would start practising with their orchestra at seven in the morning. They stuck to their commitments; if they said they would take four days for a song, they would be ready with the lyrics and the tune on the fourth day. Any musician who was not punctual would be promptly removed from their group. No one outside the two knew who had given the tune for a particular song, but they generally divided the work among themselves, each contributing half of the songs. They would divide the money, too, accordingly. Both were equally creative.

Kahin Aur Chal was more than half ready, with only twenty days of work remaining, but financier Tolaram was not willing to pay anyone. Jal Mistry was an expert cameraman and a good man at heart, but Tolaram was not willing to loosen his purse strings. Tolaram, whose intention was to avoid tax, wanted the movie to fail. Soon, staff started demanding their dues.

Shankar requested Goldie for payment, having completed four songs. Goldie asked him to demand the same from Tolaram. Asha Parekh came with the same demand. Goldie was in trouble as he himself had not received anything. Jal

Mistry had given all the rights to Tolaram, so the financier alone could help.

Dev had already had an unpleasant experience with Tolaram while working for a movie at Filmistan. He needed money to buy a house and a car, and went to get his dues from Tolaram.

'Come to my house,' Tolaram had said.

Dev reached his house to find Tolaram enjoying a leisurely massage. After a while, the financier stood up, wrapped a towel around his waist, and gave the money to Dev. Goldie had shot a few songs and a couple of sequences, but Tolaram, unwilling to pay, did not demand further dates. He could have taken Goldie into confidence, but he did not do that. Finally, Goldie managed to complete the rest of the shooting using duplicate actors. Dubbing artists did their job in place of the actors. The film was released for a day, with just the matinee show screened. Goldie was deeply hurt. It was another disturbing event in his life.

❖❖❖

Once *Hum Dono* was selected for the Berlin International Film Festival, Dev's expectations and aspirations grew. He wanted his films to do well in India and abroad. He did meet a host of directors and producers at the Berlin festival, including American producer Tad Danielewski.

When the Nobel Prize-winning author, Pearl S. Buck, visited India, she had met Dev, and discussed the possibility of making a film as an Indo-American production. Pearl was sure that the American audiences would love a stylish, suave, good-looking Indian actor like Dev Anand. She wanted to make a film on Balachandra Raja's book *Too Long in the West,* but Dev thought it too woman-centric.

His eyes fell on R.K. Narayan's novel *The Guide* at an airport bookshop – aha! He rushed to America, met Pearl and discussed film possibilities. Pearl wanted that the film have an Indian context, be made in India with its premiere in America. The American unit would only have a minor role in the whole process. Dev was going to produce the film himself and the American producers were to pay only for the negatives and bear the cost of the premiere in America. Dev argued that the cost be borne equally. Hence, it was decided that the film would be a co-production and the film would be made in English and Hindi. Dev made Pearl read *The Guide* and she, too, loved it. The book had won the Sahitya Akademi Award during Jawahar Lal Nehru's time. *The Guide* was to be made by Navketan International and Stratton Productions, New York. Pearl wanted the director of the English version to shoot it in India, whereas Dev wanted Goldie to take complete responsibility of both the versions. Goldie was reluctant to direct the film abroad. How could he relate to the culture of a country whose language he was not familiar with? So finally, it was decided that Tad Danielewski would shoot scenes of the English version and, simultaneously, the same scenes would be shot in Hindi as well.

One day Dev told Goldie, 'Pearl and the director have both liked R.K. Narayan's novel. You, too, should read it once.'

On reading, Goldie felt it would not make a great film. He found the subject cheap. According to him, if an international film was to be made in India, it should reflect Indian culture. Goldie agreed that R.K. Narayan was a great writer, but his literature was popular only among the sophisticated English writers. He also felt that the heroine falls in love with the hero, Raju, too fast. Goldie expressed his views to Dev openly.

'You can get a much better story than this one. This story is not suitable for western audiences and will not work in India. All three characters, Marco, Rosie and Raju, are negative characters and flawed in the eyes of Indian audiences. The fact that Rosie is already married, and the scene of her falling in love with Raju is fit only for American films.'

'Pearl has written the script. Why don't you read it once?' Dev suggested.

Goldie just did not like Pearl's screenplay. He wasn't keen on spending a lot of time to make the film in India. And what about Dev's reputation if the film was a flop?

'Let's make only the English version.'

'How is that possible? I will not be able to recover my investment with only one version. I have to invest a lot of money on this project. The American unit will stay here for six to eight weeks, and I will have to give them a royal treatment. We never spend so much on our films. I am not sure if I will earn enough from the English version. I have to cover my expenses with the Hindi version,' Dev explained.

'What about the songs and the music? Rosie's character is a dancer.'

'We will shoot the songs later,' Dev said.

'Can we change anything in the screenplay?' Goldie asked.

'No. Their producer has approved it and so we have to shoot it exactly the same way.'

'But once the shooting starts, who will take the first shot? The Indian director or the foreign director?'

'Yaar, they are our guests – they have to take the first shot. Then another similar shot will be taken,' said Dev.

'Then let's give them an Indian assistant who will translate the whole script into Hindi. They can shoot a scene in English and the same in Hindi as well.'

'Why do we need a director for the Hindi version? This is very demeaning for the person. The camera position, the trolley, the location selection and casting will be done by them and the Indian director will just follow them like an ass!' Goldie could not tell Dev frankly that he was against this experiment. He wasn't interested in shooting a film in the manner suggested. He did say one thing clearly,

'You may take someone else as director.'

Dev was hurt by Goldie's adamance.

'You are refusing when I need you! We will re-shoot some parts of the Hindi version later,' Dev tried to convince Goldie.

'I don't think it suits me.'

The matter rested for a while. Dev did not take Goldie's reservations seriously. Tad and his unit arrived in India, and were shown a lot of Indian films. Then the discussion on the cast began. Dev wanted to cast Vyjayanthimala, as the heroine in the film was a dancer, but Tad watched one of her films and found her unsuitable.

'But she is a famous artist, a famous dancer...'

'For my audience she is very fat. Oh my God! It would not work in America. People will not like her at all.'

After meeting a lot of actresses, Tad chose Leela Naidu. She was slim and spoke English very well. That was a big plus point for Tad.

'I want to cast her.'

Dev hit his head with his palms in frustration.

'My film will not get sold at all. Leela Naidu is not a star and cannot dance.'

'I don't intend to have any dance scenes,' Tad clarified.

'But the heroine is a dancer!'

'I am just going to show paper cuttings of her dances. I am not going to have any dances in the film,' Tad insisted.

'Tad, I will lose everything. I have to raise finances for the film and for that I need to cast a good actress,' Dev asserted.

The hunt for the actress began once again. Waheeda Rehman's name cropped up. Although she wasn't as well-known a dancer as Vyjayanthimala, she was a trained dancer. Waheeda immediately agreed to do the film.

Waheeda was Dev's selection and while Tad did not like her, he reluctantly agreed.

The Guide was a story based in a small town in South India. Most of R.K. Narayan's works were set in Malgudi, a fictional town in South India. When they spoke to R.K. Narayan, he insisted that the film be based in South India.

'Yes, we should be authentic.' Tad nodded in agreement.

'Listen, Tad, I have a very North Indian face. It will not suit a South Indian context. I will look very different among them. Most South Indians and the stars are dark-skinned and their features are very different. Why do you want to show such an image of India? We should go to a place where there is more beauty and architecture, the crowds more colourful. If you go to South India, you will find people wearing only white lungis,' Dev said.

'Then take me to North India,' said Tad and the team came to Rajasthan. Tad was happy seeing the locations.

As the project took shape, Goldie became more and more agitated. He was just not interested in the project. It was as if Tad had the last word in everything. For a farmer's role in the film, Tad chose K.N. Singh, the famous villain of Hindi films. Tad justified his selection by saying that an actor with a big build was needed for a farmer's role.

'Do you know that Indian farmers are thin and wiry men? Also, K.N. Singh is an actor who plays negative characters in Hindi films. His looks suit those roles. The moment he enters the scene, the audience will think that the villain has made his entry,' Goldie tried explaining.

Seeing Tad's perspectives and style of work, Goldie went to Dev and said, 'I cannot work on this film. I do not agree with the way Tad is going about doing things.'

Dev was shocked. He knew of Goldie's reluctance from the beginning, but was hoping he would agree to do the film. Goldie stood his ground even when some of the Navketan staff tried to convince him.

'I will not do this film. My heart is not in it. I have not become a director to work like this. Why should I work as Tad's assistant? If it was John Ford, Frank Capra, William Wyler or Alfred Hitchcock, I would have thought about it, but who is Tad? What films has he made?'

Tad's career background was nothing exceptional. He had made a few films for American television.

Goldie was exasperated and asked, 'Should I work with a man who sees an Indian farmer in K.N. Singh?'

An incensed Dev stopped talking to Goldie. Filled with anger, he asked Raj Khosla to work as Tad's assistant. Raj Khosla was elated to get a chance to work with Navketan again. He surveyed all the locations in Rajasthan with Tad. Raj decided that he would do what Dev or Tad asked him to do. It was unanimously decided that they would work on the songs later. Preparations for the shooting began, and the dress designers and art directors got down to work. Waheeda hadn't yet heard the news that Raj Khosla was going to be a part of the Hindi version till the Navketan staff went to her for fixing her dates. She called Dev and said bluntly, 'Dev, I cannot work with Raj Khosla.'

'Why?'

'I cannot tell you the reason. I am not asking you to change the director. You please choose some other actress for your film.'

Dev Anand and Waheeda Rehman were a popular pair in Hindi films, having worked together in successful films like *Kala Bazar, Solva Saal* etc. They had become close friends. He asked her gently, 'Waheeda, please tell me clearly why you are taking such a decision.'

'Raj Khosla had insulted me very badly once. I was very new in the industry then. My mother had taken a dying promise from me that I will never work with this man in my life.' It was true that Raj Khosla had said unpleasant things about Waheeda while making *Solva Saal*.

Dev was in a fix. When he mentioned Waheeda's decision to Raj Khosla, he said, 'This is not a big project for me. You don't need to change the actress for my sake. Waheeda's career is on the wane and she has got a big film after a long time. Tad agreed to cast her with great difficulty. He will not be satisfied even if you show him ten other actresses. Let Waheeda be there. If she is upset with me, I am ready to apologize to her. I can't imagine that something I said hurt her so badly.'

'Please, Dev, I neither want to meet Raj Khosla, nor do I want his apology. I don't want to talk about this to him.'

Waheeda agreed to work only if Raj Khosla left the film.

The issue of who would direct the film cropped up yet again. The Anands could think of only one name – Chetan

Anand. Chetan was busy planning to make *Haqeeqat* at that time. He had asked for permission from the Indian Army to shoot the film, but was waiting for a green signal from the central government, Punjab government and the armed forces. Seeing Dev's problem, he agreed to come on board.

Chetan decided to shoot some scenes; Tad agreed with the suggestion. Chetan wanted Goldie to rewrite some scenes, but Goldie flatly refused.

Chetan, Goldie and some others went to Udaipur to see the location. On returning to Bombay, Chetan got the letter granting necessary permissions to shoot *Haqeeqat*. The letter said he should start shooting in Ladakh immediately as it would snow later, making it impossible for trucks and jeeps to move. Chetan was not ready to let go of this opportunity – *Haqeeqat* was his dream project. He told Dev, 'Pardon me, I cannot let this chance go. I have to complete the shooting in the next six months.' Realizing that Chetan had a genuine problem at hand, Dev let him go.

He had to return to Goldie now. 'I am in a soup. I promise that you will be allowed to make the film exactly the way you want.'

Goldie was in a dilemma. He could empathize with the problem, but was not ready to compromise on his craft and talent.

'Listen, Papa, let Tad complete his shooting the way he wants. I will write a new script for *Guide* and shoot it my way. I promise you that I will take the same time that Tad takes to complete the film. I will shoot the songs along with the film and not later, because the songs will be linked to the scenes. If you want me to make *Guide,* I will do it my way,' Goldie said firmly.

Dev agreed. Tad spent money recklessly, and left for America with his unit after completing the shooting in six weeks. Goldie went to Khandala and sat in a hotel to rewrite the entire script in eighteen days.

Having recovered from a kidney problem, Goldie grew

interested in spirituality and read a lot of scriptures. He began introspecting and researching deeply about birth, death, good and bad karma. He wanted to weave aspects of his spiritual search into the film. He felt he could show how the hero of the film evolves spiritually by the end of it.

In the film, the protagonist Raju, a tourist guide, is a sinner and had been to jail. When he comes out of prison, he sees a road in Udaipur that leads to Anjanpur, literally meaning 'unknown place'. Goldie had deliberately named it thus, because Raju was clueless about his destination and his future. Spirituality is a journey that man takes towards the unknown. He finds situations that beat him, crush him and squeeze the spirituality out of him. Goldie wanted to give this message through *Guide*. He had placed a song *Wahan kaun hai tera* to suit the situation.

Goldie had shot this song on the Srinagar-Delhi highway. Raju, with a flowing beard, with thorns pricking his feet, walks on the road. He doesn't know why tears flow down his eyes or where he is headed to. Fortunately, he reaches a temple where the priest gives the freezing and shivering Raju a shawl and takes him inside. It is destiny that takes him there.

Goldie was in search of the ideal woman and, hence, introduced all the characteristics of an ideal woman in Rosie's character. These were not there in the original story.

Raju the guide is not only a guy who shows people the tourist spots of Udaipur, he is also a guide in Rosie's life. He is a spiritual guide who searches for the meaning and philosophy of life. Later, he too finds the need for someone to guide him on the spiritual path. Goldie wrote this dual track which did not exist in the original. He had read R.K. Narayan's original story only once and didn't base his script on it. Just like he made alterations to the original script, he made changes in the casting Tad had done. The era of colour films had just begun when the making of *Guide* was in progress. While making black and white films, the camera had to create the desired effects by lowering and increasing the intensity of lights. But while making colour films, the makeup and the colour combinations of the actors' clothes were important. So Dev bought costumes worth ₹2 lakhs and gave them to the costume designer, Vasant Desai, and asked him to learn costume designing. At that time, colour printing was not possible in India and the negatives of *Guide* were to be printed in a lab in the US.

It was certain that S.D. Burman would be the music director, but just before he could start work Burman suffered a heart attack and had to be hospitalized. Dev made it clear to S.D. Burman and Goldie that he was ready to wait for as long as necessary; only Sachin da was to do the music.

Sachin da's songs and Shailendra's lyrics played a major role in the success of *Guide*. Shailendra's entry into the film is an interesting story. Hasrat Jaipuri was the first choice for writing the songs, and one song written by him had been recorded too, but everyone felt that lyrics needed a little change.

'Hasrat ji, this song hasn't come out the way we wanted. It needs to be reworded,' S.D. Burman suggested. Annoyed at being rejected, Hasrat said in a demeaning manner, 'What better can I write for a pimp's character?'

Goldie and Dev were shocked when they heard this. S.D. Burman too was very hurt by Hasrat's reaction. The song had been recorded and money spent.

'How can we work with such a person?' Goldie wondered.

'What are the association rules? I don't want to work with this lyricist anymore,' Dev Anand asked. According to association rules, once a song is recorded, the lyricist had to be paid in full as per the contract.

In those days the lyricists were paid ₹500 for a song but Dev sent a cheque for ₹25,000 to Hasrat.

An apologetic Hasrat came running to the Navketan office, but Dev would have none of it.

'Hasrat ji, I cannot work with you. You don't like the theme of my film. What is the point in us working together? If I need you in future, I will let you know.'

Hasrat walked away quietly. When Shailendra got to know that Navketan was in search of a new lyricist, he called Dev directly. He had worked with Dev and Goldie in *Kala Bazar* earlier, and had become good friends with them. Goldie and Shailendra had a lot of respect for each other. Goldie believed there wasn't, and never will be, another lyricist who understood the situation better and wrote a song as fast as Shailendra. He had the capacity to write the most meaningful songs, using the simplest of words. Sahir Ludhianvi was close, but according to Goldie, Sahir's own distress reflected in his writing and his views clouded the character. Sahir could also be arrogant. In contrast, Shailendra was a simple gentleman. Goldie had a lot in common with Shailendra. He would understand the situation and context very fast. Shailendra would just go to the beach for a while to muse on the words. Even his dummy words would fit into the music score.

Goldie, Dev and Shailendra had a meeting over the song that Hasrat had written. S.D. Burman (Sachin da) came in at around 11 p.m. and the first song got ready then and there. The song was *Din dhal jaye, haye raat na jaye*. Jaidev and R.D. Burman, Sachin da's son, too were there, and the tune was ready in a jiffy.

So much meaning was expressed in that one line: *Din dhal jaye, haye raat na jaye*!

Goldie had explained the situation to S.D. Burman and Shailendra for the song, *Aaj phir jeene ki tamanna hai*. Rosie's husband had banished music, dance and art from her life. When she realizes that it was her mistake to have let go off her dance and music, she breaks all her shackles and wears her ghungaroos. The anklet bells are symbols of her freedom. She walks with gay abandon, running, dancing and prancing without any inhibitions, the bells around her ankles jingling.

Once Goldie finished explaining, S. D. Burman said, 'It's fine if you leave. The two of us will work on the song.' An hour after Goldie left, he received a call from Sachin da saying, 'The first line is ready.'

Aaj phir jeene ki tamanna hai, aaj phir marne ka irada hai...

'Wow! Next?'

Shailendra couldn't think of the lines to followed immediately.

Goldie went to Shailendra's house after a few days.

'Shailendra ji, a lot of time is getting wasted. What is the matter with you?'

'I don't know. It is all upside down. She talks of wanting to live and is determined to die?

'You can then give the reason for it in the next stanza.'

Shailendra immediately responded with, *kaanton se kheench ke ye aanchal, todke bandhan baandhi paayal...*

And the line, *aaj phir jeene,* followed.

Goldie realized that it wasn't easy writing such lyrics; only poets like Kabir Das could do it.

Kishore Kumar was in America at the time, so Sachin da got Mohammad Rafi to sing the song. But the romantic song, *Gata rahe mera dil,* was sung by Kishore once he was back.

The very popular dance-director duo of Hiralal-Sohanlal was chosen for *Guide*. Waheeda was a trained classical dancer, but she hadn't practised for long. 'I will rehearse as much as you want,' Waheeda assured Goldie. Hiralal brushed up Waheeda's dancing skills for a month before the shooting began. The practice would start at 3 a.m. and Waheeda had to take special care of her diet and nutrition.

The shooting was supposed to begin in Udaipur on 27 January. Two Mitchell cameras, trolleys, a thousand yards of electric wire, fifteen arc lamps, a hundred-yard wooden platform and other equipment were assembled. The whole unit was cooperating very well. Goldie was aware that he was competing with an American director and there would be comparisons. Not only Goldie, but the entire Hindi film industry would be compared with Hollywood, and Goldie was making the film with a vengeance. *Guide* was not a commercial subject and Goldie had a free hand in adapting it his own way. Goldie was conscious that the aesthetics of the film shouldn't be compromised and even if people didn't appreciate the spiritual angle of the film, the music and dances should help the film sail through. That is why he worked on both the content and the commercial aspects of the film.

Moreover, Tad's film was going to be premiered in New York and was to be exhibited in several international film festivals. Many Indians living abroad would watch the film.

Goldie knew that the Hindi version would not be released abroad, but even if it was released only in India, many people will have the opportunity to watch both the versions. In which case, they should find his version superior! Goldie had found that Tad wasn't very creative and his feeling was proven right when he watched rushes of what Tad had shot. He had made a very superficial film and not understood the depth of the story. Goldie had decided that he was going to make an intense film and create history of sorts in Indian films. He wasn't worried about the success or failure of the film right from the beginning; he hadn't come into the film industry in search of fame or money.

In the initial days of the shooting, the cameraman, Fali Mistry, tried too hard to embellish the scenes. Once while preparing to shoot a foreground scene, he suddenly asked his assistant to get some flowers. When Goldie saw the scene, he didn't like the setting. The scene required a simple background where a man is walking alone, depicting his loneliness. Goldie felt that the flowers were dominating the frame. The flowers could have worked for a still photograph, but not the film. He told Fali, 'I have placed the camera here because I wanted a wide-angle view. The flowers are restricting the view and diverting the attention from the character. Please remove the flowers.'

Fali agreed and stopped decorating frames in future. Goldie was trying to show an internal conflict, which was very difficult to display on screen. Directors used either a voice-over or dialogues to present it, but Goldie wanted to highlight the emotions. Fali would discuss with Goldie before setting up his camera and Goldie, too, would suggest different colour screens to depict the right mood.

For example, as Raju's sainthood strengthens, the sunflower yellow colour, too, darkens. Goldie would tell the art director the background colour and the shade Fali wanted for a particular scene. And because of this, the dress designer and the art director worked enthusiastically.

Goldie had heard that the legendary director V. Shantaram was too dominating on the sets, while Mehboob Khan gave his cameraman a free hand. Mehboob would call Naushad Ali, the music director, tell him the storyline and ask him to make songs to suit the situations. Naushad would suggest the places where songs would fit and compose the songs accordingly. Goldie did not like either style – one director dominating the unit completely and the other director ready to give up his own perceptions and conceptions to work on others' opinions. It was important to opt for a middle path because filmmaking was about teamwork, and one needed to get the opinions of not only the technicians, like the cameraman, art director, lightman, actors, lyricist and music director, but also the trolley man and other ordinary assistants. Each of them was the director's tools and they had their own ideas, strengths and weaknesses. It was vital for the director to leverage their strengths. Goldie worked with complete consensus, and never came home from the sets disappointed or stressed.

There were two occasions, though, when Dev and Goldie had disagreements. One was during the shooting of the song *Din dhal jaye, haye raat na jaye*. While the song played in the background, Rosie walks down the staircase, and Raju stands with eyes shut at the bottom of the steps, holding the banister. Rosie's hand comes close to Raju's, but she hesitates to touch him. While shooting this scene, Dev believed it was important for Rosie to touch Raju because she still loved him, but Goldie disagreed. The shooting had to be halted because the brothers didn't agree with each other.

Rosie loved Raju wholeheartedly, but had got estranged lately because of his behaviour. She disliked his deceit, his dishonesty, money laundering, thievery and drinking habits.

And that is why Goldie felt that their hands should not touch in that scene. If she had to be shown holding his hand, it should have been after he comes out of jail, but Raju goes to Anjanpur once he is released from jail and his life changes. This was an important scene in the film. A director looks at the storyline and the forthcoming scenes, whereas the actor thinks only about a particular scene. Goldie convinced Dev and shooting resumed.

In the end of the film, Raju the guide becomes an ascetic, and fasts for twelve days to pray for rains. In one of the scenes, Goldie wanted to show Raju with a beard, weak and drained. He didn't want Dev's face to look handsome and told Fali discreetly, 'Make him ugly.'

Dev didn't like it when he heard about this. 'Never make a star ugly. His stardom will be ruined.'

Dev had, after all, cultivated and maintained his chocolate-boy image for years.

Goldie countered, 'I want to make an ugly Dev Anand become more beautiful. The contrast will increase. Once he becomes an ascetic, Raju's ego will be destroyed, and I will use lenses that will destroy his face.'

Goldie instructed Dev's makeup man to make Dev as dark as possible. Dev was upset and protested.

'The shot is ready,' Goldie announced.

Dev refused to come out of the makeup van. When Goldie asked, the makeup man said that Dev had not yet got his makeup done. A cold war was on! Fali went to Goldie and said, 'Hey, what he says is also correct. Dev Anand is a big star. Why don't you adjust a little?'

'No! That way the film will lose its essence. He needs time to be convinced. The moment he is convinced, he himself will get the makeup done,' Goldie said.

That is exactly what happened. As expected, Dev came out with full makeup on. He behaved as if nothing had happened and he didn't say anything after he saw the trial shot on the screen. But Goldie knew that Dev liked the shot.

Goldie's father, Pishorimal

Goldie's mother

Goldie – talented and creative, yet lonely

A gathering of creative minds at Chetan Anand's home. S.D. Burman, Balraj Sahani, Zohra Sehgal, Chetan and Dev Anand, with young Goldie

A photo of Goldie with his college friends

On the set of *Nau Do Gyarah*, with Shashikala, Lalita Pawar, Zohra Sehgal and other members of the film-unit

With Waheeda Rehman in *Kala Bazaar*, which he directed as well as acted in

Dev Anand and Nutan in *Tere Grah Ke Samne*, for which Goldie wrote the screenplay

(L to R) R.D. Burman, Dev Anand, S.D. Burmanand Hasrat Jaipuri, seen during a music composing session for *Guide*

Director Goldie explaining a scene to Waheeda Rehman during the filming of the iconic song, *Aaj phir jeene ki tamanna hai...* in *Guide*

A milestone in the annals of Hindi cinema...
Dev Anand and Waheeda Rehman in *Guide*

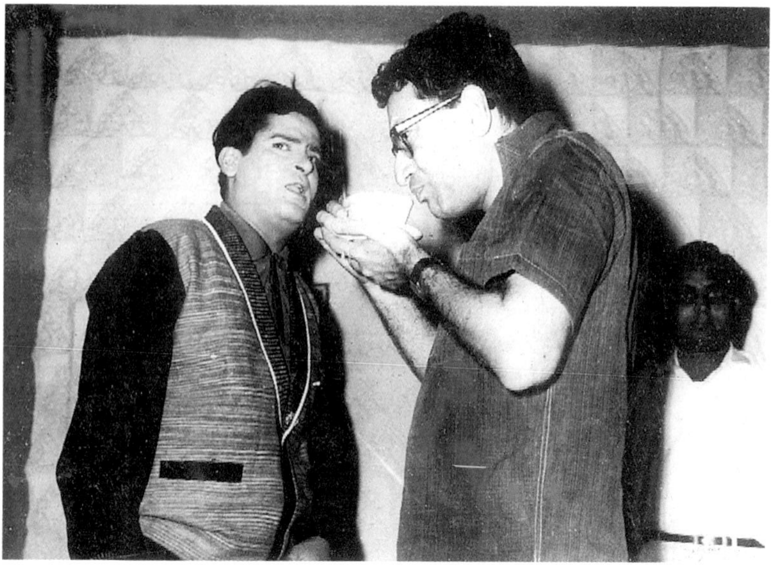

Shammi Kapoor and Goldie on the sets of *Teesri Manzil*

Goldie and Nasir Hussain during the filming of *Teesri Manzil*

Goldie actually directed the movie *Hum Dono*, but Amarjeet got the credit as the director, on screen

Goldie and Dev Anand at the premier of *Jewel Thief*

Ashok Kumar, Goldie and Dev Anand celebrating
at the premier of *Jewel Thief*

(L to R) Sapru, Ashok Kumar, Vaijayanthimala and
Dev Anand during the filming of *Jewel Thief*

For the song *Piya tose naina lage re,* shot in an open auditorium in Udaipur, Goldie erected nine different sets for the nine-minute long dance sequence. He shot the song *Tere mere sapne ab ek rang hain* near a beautiful lake. Since the sunrise lasted only for eight minutes, he couldn't get the scene right. The brightness of the light was uneven and finally Goldie and the art director, Ram Yedekar, stood under the shade of a tree and shot the song with the desired background. Goldie had his own characteristic way of shooting songs. Dance directors were responsible only for the dance steps, while Goldie himself decided the camera angles, song situation and movement.

The climax of the film was shot in Limdi where the set of a temple was erected on the empty grounds of an old palace near the railway station. In one of the scenes, a woman places her dead child before Raju, who is fasting, and asks him to bring the child back to life. But Raju was not capable of miracles. A prayer rises in Raju's mind for the first time, seeing the woman's sorrow. Tears flow down his face, and fall on the child's body. Dev really cried in that scene; not a single dry eye on the set that day!

Goldie was thrilled by the performance of the junior artistes for the *He Ram* song. They had understood the situation and the scene very well. The song's shoot proved that irrespective of religion, human feelings were the same. The sky had turned cloudy, so Goldie quickly completed the shoot. It did rain later, but the shooting was over by then.

Waheeda had a genial personality and her face didn't show expressions powerfully. Goldie found it difficult to capture her reactions properly during the shoot. To make her performance high and robust during the shooting of the song, *Aaj phir jeene ki tamanna hai,* Goldie kept Devs profile low and used a lot of props like camels and trucks.

Dev had borrowed ₹6 lakhs for the film. A few of his well-wishers wondered if the movie would bankrupt him. (It was partly true; Dev did not recover a penny from the English version. Had Goldie not made the Hindi version his way, Dev would have lost all his money).

The news that *Guide* was not a commercial film had spread like wildfire in the film industry, and the distributors were annoyed that Dev 'dies' at the end of the film. *Guide* was the only Navketan film that didn't get sold during the making or immediately after it was ready.

A distributor from Bengal told Goldie, 'Please change the climax of the film. Don't let Dev Anand sahab die.' Goldie bluntly refused.

Despite being a story about an extra-marital relationship, Goldie did not show Raju and Rosie coming together in the end. When Rosie meets Raju in the end, he is an ascetic. Goldie showed them going their separate ways, keeping Indian sensibilities in mind. Once a man renounces the world, he cannot return to regular domestic life.

Dev wanted to portray Rosie pregnant with Raju's child when the starving and weak Raju is admitted to hospital after it rains. But Goldie put his foot down and refused. Because of the mixed reactions from the distributors, Dev stopped showing the film to them, but he had complete confidence in Goldie's hard work and his capabilities as a director. A distributor from Delhi wanted to watch the film. Producer Yash Johar was working as a production controller with Navketan those days.

He told Goldie, 'Why don't you allow the Delhi distributor to see a few songs?'

Goldie showed two songs, *Piya tose naina lage re* and *Gaata rahe mera dil,* to the distributor without Dev's knowledge. The distributor was stunned.

'No one has screened such songs before. Why are you hesitant? I am buying your movie,' the distributor said. Soon, other distributors started enquiring.

The movie was screened for a select audience. Many of the people associated with the industry came, watched the movie and went away without saying a word. There was no reaction – good or bad! It was the same during the movie's premiere at the Maratha Mandir Theatre in Mumbai. Those days premiere shows used to be celebrated like a wedding function. But the atmosphere after the premiere of *Guide* reminded one of a funeral!

After the premier, everyone returned to Dev's home while Amarjeet, who looked after the publicity, started calling people who had attended the premiere. B.R. Chopra, the famous producer-director said bluntly, 'I couldn't understand head or tail of it!'

Many others, too, expressed similar opinion. Everyone was depressed. The monsoon season had begun, but it had not started raining heavily. After ten weeks of the premiere, Dev released an advertisement in *Screen,* a weekly film magazine: '*Guide* prays for rain.' And surprisingly, it poured soon thereafter!

The film started getting positive reviews, slowly – over weeks and months and over the years now. The initial reactions of a 'good movie' soon became 'very good.' Today it is hailed as a classic.

Had they not competed with the American producers, they probably would not have got such fantastic results. Goldie had the courage to make a movie which stood apart from others. It was probably destiny; people like Raj Khosla and Chetan Anand had tried their hand at making *Guide,* but finally it was for Goldie to make it. Had Goldie agreed with Dev to make the movie with the American producer, it would have been of a poor quality.

For nearly five years after the making of *Guide,* Goldie had turned an ascetic himself. His spiritual bent of mind was reflected in the making of *Guide.* The movie catapulted Goldie to the list of top directors of India, but Dev received far more acclaim as a star actor. Dev now had a halo around him. Reporters vied to interview him. On the other hand, Goldie could never establish that kind of relationship with the press or publicise himself. He did not believe in beating his own drum, preferring to be behind the camera.

In the English version of *Guide,* Dev is his usual self that people see in many movies, but he comes across entirely different in the Hindi version. Goldie was confident of his brother's capabilities. Dev and Waheeda received the *Filmfare* best actor and actress award; Goldie bagged the screenplay and editing awards, R.K. Narayan the best story award. The film bagged seven *Filmfare* awards. Surprisingly, S.D. Burman was not even nominated for the award. Goldie told the story of how it happened.

The award committee met S.D. Burman a day before the award ceremony and demanded money for the award. As expected, Burman da asked the men to get out of his house. The men then reached out to Goldie, demanding ₹50,000 for the best director award. They were thrown out again.

Goldie asked them if they had other names in mind for the award. When Goldie heard the names, he called the other directors and warned them of such a plan. 'You may pay them if you wish to buy the award,' he told them.

The news spread all over and in order to save face, the committee ensured that *Guide* received all the awards it deserved.

Goldie always resented the fact that S.D. Burman was not awarded. Well, the music of *Guide* is beyond any award and is evergreen. It does not require the stamp and seal of any awards.

While *Guide* was winning accolades all over, R.K. Narayan, the original writer who had initially praised the rushes, gave an interview to *Life*, the American magazine, a year after the release of the movie, trashing it.

'They have done great injustice to me by changing the story without consulting me. I don't like that at all,' he complained.

When the movie was released, the same writer had sent letters congratulating Dev. He had said that the accolades for the film were a compliment to the novel. He had personally told Waheeda how much he had enjoyed the film. Dev, taken aback at R.K. Narayan's change of heart, publicly asked,

'Why didn't he express his opinion when he saw the movie? How did he accept the best-story award? Why was he silent then?'

R.K. Narayan did not reply. The fact was that both Goldie and Dev had consulted the author and kept him abreast of the changes they were making.

Dev had signed a contract for the other version of *Guide* with Pearl S. Buck. As per the contract, he was to take care of the expenses in India while the distribution in the US was her responsibility. The colour stock came from the US and for printing and processing, Goldie and his team had to go there.

By the time the Hindi version was being readied, the English version was screened in New York. Dev attended the premiere, which did not see much success. Dev agreed that the English version was 'artificial' and 'superficial' compared to the Hindi one. The English version was a flop, and those associated with it did not met Goldie or Dev when they were in the US for the editing and related work. They had to, thus, bear all the expenses. It was an unfortunate outcome of the whole affair.

Meanwhile, the Indian Film Producers' Association and the central government nominated *Guide* as India's official entry for the Oscars. Goldie and Dev once again left for the US. Dev had a lot of friends in New York. One of them was a popular author who liked the movie very much, and introduced Dev to a producer with MGM Studios who also liked *Guide*.

'This movie can win the Oscar in the foreign films category, but you need to do a few things. It is important that all the members of the Academy see the film. Movie makers from Italy, France and Japan spend a lot of money on publicity, hosting parties, making friends with people in the Academy and Hollywood. They invite each member of the Academy personally. If you want to do all this, you need to stay here for a fortnight at least. Else, you are likely to get very few votes. It would be a tragedy that after making such a good movie, you don't take advantage of it,' the producer advised.

The producer also suggested taking a fresh look at the subtitles. He believed the Indian way of subtitles may not appeal to the American viewer.

Sir David Lean, the famous producer-director, had liked *Guide*. He told Goldie,

'You are young and have a lot of potential on the international stage. If I could, I would select *Guide* for the best picture. But if you do get that, I would like to sign you up.'

'I am not keen to be an international director. I also believe we are unlikely to get the award,' Goldie said, politely rejecting the offer.

Due to a paucity of funds, it was not possible to get *Guide* the kind of publicity required to make a mark. Goldie felt dejected. He wondered if a good movie alone was enough unless it was backed by adequate publicity. Till the Indian producers did this, it would be impossible to capture the international market. Making a movie was different from promoting it. And that required a completely different set-up supported by adequate funds. Dev and Goldie did try their best to promote the film. But it was impossible to make an impact without spending money and the Indian government did not provide any such support. Staying in Hollywood was expensive; the brothers spent a few days there, and the rest of the fortnight in New York. Unlike the Berlin festival, where Dev and Goldie made friends with a lot of international producers and directors, they did not get an opportunity in Hollywood with *Guide*.

Upon return to India, they handed over the print to someone. They did not even know how many of the Academy members saw the film or the number of votes it got. Dev was convinced that publicity would have fetched *Guide* an Oscar.

During *Nau Do Gyarah* Goldie's monthly salary was ₹500, which was raised to ₹1,000 after *Kala Bazar*. Goldie received a mere ₹5,000 for *Guide*; that too on the recommendation of Yash Johar. Goldie, though, never asked Dev for money.

Even a cursory glance at, an example of experimental filmmaking, reveals it as a commercial film with an artistic angle to it. Each time the viewer finds something different.

All the three characters in the film are negative. The heroine, Rosie, leaves her husband to have an affair with Raju the guide. Rosie earns a lot of money through her dances even as Raju enjoys the newfound luxury. Marco, Rosie's husband, ill-treated her as she was a devdasi's daughter. He cheated on her. Yet, all the characters are not totally negative. Keeping in mind that a woman having an extra-marital affair may not appeal to the viewers, she is shown to have a deep love for dance. Goldie conveys her husband's shabby treatment of her via the famous snake dance.

Goldie used long sequences in only a few places. One was when Rosie and Marco argue; Rosie has just found him with another woman. The other scene is when the villagers beat Raju, and the guide turns into a sadhu. The third scene is when Raju, now trapped as a sadhu, indulges in a soliloquy. He ponders over the existence of God, and whether he would be able to live up to the faith of the villagers and produce rain. He uses scenes ranging from a few seconds to a few minutes to familiarise viewers with the timelines and in order to build continuity in the narrative.

For example, in an initial scene Raju is shown coming out of a prison. Guilt and remorse reflect on his face, and he is hesitant to go back to his village to face his mother. A short flashback of a few minutes shows Raju's character, his mother, house and the beautiful tourist spots of Udaipur where he worked as a guide. We come to know of the smart 'Raju guide' who knows how to win his customers.

Raju remains practical-minded even as he turns to spirituality. Remember that scene when Raju talks to Rosie as she tries to commit suicide?

'If this is the limit of your courage, then every woman will be ashamed of you... Marco was unhappy but he did not go and bang his head on the wall. Instead, he found solace in caves, talking to statues and rocks. Only because he is a man? And you are torturing yourself – because you are a woman? This is not right, Rosie... It's not right, you suffering because of this.'

Rosie sits with her face covered. Raju comes into close-up.

'This is because you have not learnt to revolt against your situation.'

Rosie lifts her head to look.... Close-up of Rosie's face.

Mid-long shot. Rosie is on the bed. Raju standing near the bed.

'It is a sin to tolerate torture. It is a sin to accept defeat. And to live life suffocating yourself.'

Many such shots develop the character of Raju. After turning into a sadhu, he starts a school, a post office and a dispensary in the village.

Goldie filmed the song, *Piya tose naina lage re,* in such a way that the story moves forward, showing Rosie's increasing popularity and the material success that Raju enjoys. Using nearly sixty-odd shots, Goldie carried the story forward with the song, *Wahan kaun hai tera,* where we see Raju travelling in buses and tongas, Rosie's photos, and Raju hobbling in torn shoes, to indicate the passage of time.

Here's another scene showcasing Goldie's talents as a director and dialogue writer:

Rosie enters the room, following a servant who carries the costume. A beautiful marble statue of a dancer is in the background. Rosie stops as she walks down the staircase when she sees Raju in his earlier avatar, wearing the dress of a tourist guide.

'Raju, is this is a joke?'

'I wish it was! The joke is that it is not a joke, Miss Nalini.'

'Why are you making a spectacle of this?'

'When I have become a spectacle myself, where is the question of creating one?'

Rosie does not believe that Raju is actually going away and asks him to come back after changing his dress. 'I will wait. Come soon.'

'I waited a lot. On a path where you never wanted to walk.'

'What's come over you?' Rosie looks at her watch and says, 'It is time for the show.'

Raju's mother and Rosie are shocked to hear that Raju has been released from jail early. Raju's mother blames Rosie when he does not return home. Rosie speaks of how they separated. This is where Goldie inserts a flashback of nearly 2 hours.

In order to show the increasing tension between Marco, Rosie and Raju, Goldie uses five- to seven-second scenes.

Raju may have been the cause of the separation between Marco and Rosie, but Marco is indebted to Raju for showing him the caves and acknowledges the same in his book. Goldie shows the good and the bad in the same man.

Sometimes a scene has no action – this is where the dialogue writer needs to show his craft. What a religious speaker is not able to tell the audience in many hours, is shown by Goldie in a few minutes. In the last twenty minutes of the film, it does not seem like Raju is giving a discourse. Goldie has shown, through his writing, the nuances of what Raju as an ascetic, experiences, be it the compassion he develops for the villagers, the change of heart, and his experiences that he shares with the people. It helped, no doubt, that Goldie had an outstanding actor like Dev to play Raju.

Songs are undoubtedly the heart of Hindi cinema. Mehboob Khan, Bimal Roy, Chopra, V. Shantaram and Raj Kapoor made songs glamorous. But it was Goldie who put songs on a pedestal. *Tere Ghar Ke Samne, Guide, Teesri Manzil, Jewel Thief*.... one can see how Goldie has given a special treatment to each of the songs in these films. It still makes one's hair stand on end.

There are directors who make an actor act in front of a camera and then add all the shots together to make a film. It was Goldie who treated each scene and actor differently. He would imagine each shot and its image size, lens used, camera movement, volume, the length of the shot, the movement of the actors, and the dialogues to fit a particular scene. Goldie was a perfect combination of a dialogue writer, director and editor. He got the best out of all, be it actors like Dev Anand, Pran, Shammi Kapoor, Waheeda Rehman, Hema Malini Mumtaz, or music directors like Jaidev, S.D. Burman, R.D. Burman, or Kalyanji-Anandji.

Goldie, being a writer himself, knew the exact meaning and location of each song in the making of the movie. Most of his songs were not inserted for the sake of it. Each scene has a dominant emotion, which is reflected through the story, situation and dialogues of the actors. The song begins when the words are not enough to describe the emotions. Goldie was clear that his songs carried the narrative forward. The song gave words and meaning to the emotions the scene unfolded.

The song is literally an extension of the dialogues before the song begins. One can see this, for example, in the song *Tere mere sapne*. It is a diamond in Goldie's repertoire. The entire song is captured in four shots. Raju and Rosie's acting, their walking near a lake, the evening sun reflecting on its surface, and the camera movement are so well-orchestrated that one can watch the song innumerable times. Same is the case with songs like *Dil ka bhanwar kare pukar* and *Main zindagi ka saath nibhata chala gayaa*.

In one of the stanzas of *Tere mere sapne*, Raju stretches his hand towards Rosie, and the camera pans towards her. The background score of saxophone and piano are simply stunning. The camera moves from Raju's hands to capture the evening light as it spreads over the distant lake. As the camera lovingly captures the beauty of the evening, it gently takes Rosie's face into the frame. It is a poetic movement on celluloid. Goldie gave his viewers many such moments to enjoy again and again. His contribution to cinema becomes even more exemplary when we compare these with the songs of today. It is our good fortune that such moments of pure delight are here for posterity.

Films like *Guide* have a depth that's rarely seen. It is a movie that aptly showcases Goldie's gift for experimenting with the medium. No other director has had the courage to do so. Which is why *Guide* holds a special place in the film industry's heart.

❖❖❖

The shooting for *Teesri Manzil* also began while *Guide* was still being produced. This was the first movie outside the Navketan banner that Goldie did.

Munimji was being directed by Subodh Mukerjee with Dev in the lead role. Nasir Hussain had played a part in writing the script. Those days if a director was not articulate or was unable to read out the script to the actors, the scriptwriter had to be on the sets to explain the scene to them. The actors may even suggest changes in the script. Subodh used to have two or three scriptwriters on the sets and selected a scene after listening to them. Hussain, having left Filmistan, had set up his own studio and decided to produce *Jab Pyaar Kisise Hota Hai* starring Dev.

This made them good friends. One day Hussain suggested that they go to Darjeeling for the shoot as it was a beautiful town. Dev readily agreed and blocked thirty days.

Hussain was not able to pay Dev and apologized. Dev asked,

'Did I ask you for money? You just get the movie ready. Don't worry about money.'

Those days a lot of filmmakers shot the climax after taking feedback from friends and relatives. Hussain, too, organized the trial for the shooting of the climax scene for *Jab Pyaar Kisise Hota Hai*. Dev asked Goldie to come along.

The next day Hussain asked Goldie, 'So how was the movie?'

'Nasir, your movie will do very well. Don't worry. The movie will be a hit.'

Hussain was thrilled. He said, 'I am keen to have another song in the movie, but not sure where to put it.'

After taking suggestions from Goldie, he added the song *Teri zulfon se judaai*. All the songs were popular and the film, a light romantic story, was received well. Hussain was especially grateful to Goldie for his comments and his advice on adding the song. It is not common for one director to praise another one or ask for his help. Impressed with Goldie, Nasir asked him if he would direct a movie outside the Navketan banner.

'I will, if Dev is part of it.'

Guide was being shot at that time. Goldie wondered why Hussain, who was a producer-director himself, wanted his help.

'Why don't you direct it yourself?' he asked.

'I want to rest a little. You direct the movie for me.'

'Sure,' said Goldie.

It was obvious that the hero would be Dev Anand. It was soon announced that Hussain was going to make a movie with Dev and Goldie. While the story was being discussed, Hussain threw a party at his house to which Dev and Goldie were invited. While the party was in full swing, people heard Dev and Hussain arguing loudly. There was pin drop silence when Dev stormed out of the party. No one, including Goldie, knew what the argument was about. Apparently, Hussain was not in agreement with Dev's view that a movie ran on the shoulders of the hero.

After a few days, Goldie heard that Dev had decided not to work with Hussain. The news spread like wildfire. The question on everyone's mind was whether Goldie would go ahead with the movie. Goldie's response was, 'Dev has not told me not to direct the movie. Nor has Nasir said that I should not direct the movie because my brother is not acting in it. It would neither be professional nor ethical on my part to walk out of the movie. I personally don't have any differences with Nasir.'

The rumours stopped. One day Nasir asked Goldie, '*Yaar,* now that Dev is not there, who do you recommend for the hero's role?' 'Let us see who is available and would be willing to work with us. I am fine with anyone.'

'I like Shammi Kapoor. We've made a hit film together.'

Hussain was referring to *Tumsa Nahin Dekha,* which had been quite successful.

Shammi readily agreed. It was a foregone conclusion that Asha Parekh would be the heroine. Goldie was comfortable working with her and believed that she made up the deficit in her acting talent with hard work. She did not have the tantrums of a heroine, and followed the director's instructions carefully.

Shammi and Goldie had never worked together. Goldie was going to work with a hero other than Dev for the first time; Shammi was happy to work with a successful director like Goldie. Shammi was a little apprehensive of the fact that Goldie worked for Navketan and that he was a star's brother.

Well, Goldie and Shammi knew each other from childhood. All actors working for Prithvi Theatre were frequent visitors to Chetan's place. Goldie had first met Shammi then.

They had met again many years later in Indore, where Goldie was shooting for *Nau Do Gyarah* on the road. They both were staying in the same hotel when Goldie spotted Shammi sitting in the garden under an umbrella. They were thrilled to meet each other. Shammi, not yet a star then, said,

'We are in the same boat.'

'How so?'

'Well, you are under the shadow of Dev Anand, while people know me as Raj Kapoor's brother. I hate my brother!'

'I suggest you be proud of him. I am, of being Dev's brother. There are advantages and disadvantages, I agree, but that's life!'

'People keep comparing the two of us,' Shammi complained.

Goldie shrugged his shoulders; he did not want to discuss this further.

Shammi and Goldie were now meeting once again thanks to Nasir Hussain's film. Shammi was a star now, and Goldie could see a new formality in his behaviour.

'Tell me the story,' Shammi said.

Goldie was yet to finalize a story, but he was certain that it had to approved by Hussain too. Goldie believed that if Hussain gave the story, he would be personally involved in the making of the film. One day Hussain said, 'Goldie, I don't have a story, but I have an incident in mind.' He described the scene:

A car, carrying two young women, stops at a petrol pump. One woman asks the other, 'Why do you want to waste your time going to Kashmir? You won't be able to meet him there.'

'But I want to go. My sister's murderer is over there. I will not sit quiet till I have taken revenge.'

'You don't even know his name or address. How do you intend to catch him?'

'I know for sure that he is known as Rocky and that he plays the drums in a local club. And he has a habit of wearing sunglasses,' she said.

Hearing this, a young man on a scooter at the petrol pump, takes off his sunglasses....

Goldie replied, 'This is not just a scene, it is a complete story with great potential. It can be made into a good movie. Let us work on the subject. I think Shammi will fit the role of the hero well. We will decide later whether he hears the girl or not, but the angle of the young woman wanting to take revenge for her sister's death is interesting.'

Hussain concurred with Goldie's view, and they started working on the script. Since the drama unfolds on the third floor of a hotel, the film was titled *Teesri Manzil*. Goldie knew that there were certain things Hussain would want included in the film as he was the producer, but Goldie had his own ideas when it came to the script. He believed in the independence of the director. Hussain had a particular format for every movie, with a hotel in each. Songs were a must and so was the heroine's friend. Goldie believed that even with all this, he could have a script that was different. Without disturbing the main storyline, Goldie started working on the script in his own style. It was clear that Hussain was to be credited for the story and screenplay. But it turned out to be *Teesri Manzil's* uniqueness that despite Hussain's typical formula and Shammi Kapoor's usual romance, the film eventually took on Goldie's style.

The hero is a drummer in a hotel – so it was obvious there *had* to be a dancer. This is where the character of Helen evolved. Instead of merely being a dancer, Goldie made her character crucial by adding the elements of her love for the drummer and being a witness to a murder. When the heroine comes searching for the hero in the hotel, the hero asks his friend to play the drums instead, thus creating the character of Salim. This was Salim of the Salim Khan-Javed Akhtar duo of ace screenwriters that would take the industry by storm in a few years time, and who was at the time aspiring to be an actor. Each supporting character in Nasir's film evolved in this manner.

Goldie wanted to give the role of the villain to an actor who had not played the role of a villain earlier, so that the viewers would not doubt him. As the role was not long, Goldie was not sure if he could get a star to play the role. At this time, Goldie came to know that the erstwhile hero Premnath was looking for a comeback role. Recalling the stage play competition in college where Premnath had given him an award, Goldie saw an opportunity to say thank you. He managed to convince the veteran actor to do this role. It is a different matter that while *Teesri Manzil* went on to become a hit, it failed to become a 'comeback' film for Premnath, unfortunately.

After the script was ready, Goldie and Hussain wanted to finalize the music director. Hussain was keen on O.P. Nayyar.

'Nasir, let us try Burman da's son, Pancham. I want to give him a break. We have decided to take him for our next film at Navketan.'

S.D. Burman had a permanent music studio at Navketan and was highly respected there. Pancham, aka R.D. Burman, was his only son and Burman da was keen that he should get a break and compose music independently. As S.D. Burman was not keeping well, he was determined to make his son well-entrenched in the industry as a music director.

When *Guide* was being shot, he had asked Goldie,

'What do you think of Pancham? Can he compose music independently?'

Goldie had promised that he would give Pancham a chance. Here was an opportunity to offer the job to Pancham.

But Hussain had his doubts about Shammi agreeing to Pancham. 'What has Shammi got to do with the selection of a music director? You are the producer and I am the director.

I have to see to it that I do justice to your money. If you are going to make a movie based on what Shammi wants, then you don't need me. Shammi, I can assure you, will be happy that the songs are to his liking,' Goldie said, making his point clear. Hussain was left dumbfounded.

Goldie clarified, 'I don't know Nayyar sahab, though I have immense respect for his music. But his music will not suit the story.'

Shammi warned him when Hussain related this to him, 'Please be careful. Soon, Goldie and Dev Anand's group will take over your company. You must keep the choice of music director under your control. Take Shankar-Jaikishan if you wish.'

Goldie told Hussain, 'I know Shankar-Jaikishan are good, but I wish to give Pancham a chance. He can make tunes that I want, unlike Shankar-Jaikishan who are too busy. Pancham will give us all the time we want. You tell Shammi that Goldie is adamant and hell-bent on Pancham.'

Hussain wanted to manage the issue tactfully. After all, Shammi was a top star those days. It was a tough act, as Goldie was, unlike Hussain, blunt and to the point. Hussain finally managed to convince Shammi, giving the excuse about Goldie wanting to stick to his guns.

Pancham was desperate for a break. He had given the music for *Chhote Nawab,* but the movie did not fare well. The music in the film was on the lines of S.D. Burman's work, and had he not got the chance to compose music for *Teesri Manzil,* he would have gone on composing in his father's style.

Goldie advised Pancham, 'If you make tunes the way Dev likes, it would not suit Shammi. You have seen his films. He likes songs where he jumps and dances all around. Compose tunes that will floor Shammi. I have pushed your name. I will arrange for a meeting with him.'

Spurred by Goldie's assurance, Pancham got down to work, composing songs based on the situations in the film. Hussain met Pancham before they were to meet Shammi. Hussain had a lot of respect for Burman da. He was sure his son would be equally talented.

Goldie told Shammi, 'You, too, must have been given a break by someone. Talent needs a chance, don't you agree? You are rejecting Pancham even before hearing him out. I suggest you hear his tunes first. If you don't like them, we will talk about taking on another music director.'

A dinner meeting was organized at Hussain's house. Pancham came with his music troupe and sat, slightly to one side. Goldie never touched alcohol but Shammi loved his drinks. While shooting for *Teesri Manzil* at Mahabaleshwar, Shammi would get upset at Goldie going for a walk instead of having a drink. 'You never have a drink with me!' Shammi would accuse.

'That is not correct. It is not that I don't have a drink with you. I don't drink, period! What is the point in my sitting here then? That is why I go and take a walk,' Goldie would explain.

During the dinner at Hussain's house, Pancham had to win Shammi's heart through his music. After downing a few pegs, Shammi asked Pancham, 'I believe you are going to play some tunes?'

Pancham and his group readied themselves. Pancham played the tune for the song, *O haseena zulfon waali*. The words were different then, of course. Shammi, determined to reject Pancham, was pleasantly surprised and smiled. He had a good ear for rhythm. Soon, Pancham had played four more of his tunes. He never realized that Shammi had quietly moved closer to him.

Shammi said, 'Why don't you give me some *pahadi* tune?'

Pancham played the tune for the song *Deewana mujh sa nahin*.

'Wah, wah!' Shammi exclaimed. That night Pancham played many of his tunes that Hussain used later in movies like *Yaadon Ki Baaraat* and *Hum Kisisse Kum Naheen*.

Duly impressed, Shammi hugged Pancham affectionately. Seeing Shammi in such a good mood, Pancham knew he had bagged the job.

Once, while Pancham was busy composing music, Asha Bhosle came to meet Goldie. Asha and Lata Mangheskar were regular singers with Navketan. The Anand brothers had good rapport with them. When she met Goldie, Asha said,

'I want you to give the music direction of this film to my sahab.' She was referring to O.P. Nayyar.

'Have you heard Pancham?' Goldie asked.

'No,' Asha replied. Goldie then explained to her why he wanted to give Pancham a break.

'You can give him a chance at Navketan. It is always O.P. Nayyar when it comes to Nasir Hussain's films,' Asha insisted.

'That might be so when Nasir directs himself. I am directing this film, so I will take one who suits my style. I have given my word to Pancham. It's not that I am insulting Nayyar sahab. His style of music will just not suit my storyline.'

Asha was insistent, but Goldie stand prevailed. Later, Nayyar gave a statement to the press that it was he who had declined Goldie's offer as the budget for the film was too small. But Goldie did not react to this. Asha sang the songs composed by Pancham for *Teesri Manzil*. As it would turn out years later, Asha and Pancham would fall in love and get married!

The shooting for the movie began in earnest. First day first shot is always a power struggle for directors and actors. While Shammi wanted to instruct Goldie, the latter wanted him to relax a bit. There is an unspoken communication between the director and the actor once the lights are on and the director is behind the camera. Goldie realized that Shammi was nervous and decided to shoot a simple scene; the shot showed only his legs as he drags his luggage to the railway ticket counter. The next shot was that of a long dialogue.

Shammi never memorized his dialogues. He would understand the essence of the dialogue and then say it in his own words. But in a long scene that was not possible. He had to memorize the lines. Shammi wanted six or seven breaks, complaining,

'*Yaar,* how do I say everything in one shot?'

Goldie gently suggested that Shammi try out different styles and to have a few rehearsals before the final shot.

In the shot, while Asha is standing at the window to buy her ticket, Shammi and she start talking as they walk to a particular spot. They were to keep looking ahead while speaking, their expressions changing with the dialogues. It was a long and difficult shot. Shammi did not want to rehearse too many times as he believed it would take away the 'natural' look.

'Not at all,' Goldie objected. 'It will make the shot perfect. A good actor continues to remain spontaneous. Don't worry.'

Goldie okayed the scene in the first take itself, much to Shammi's surprise. Shammi had come to understand that Goldie was a star master and knew how to get work done. They started off on a good wicket though they did have an argument once.

It was during the shooting of a song in Mehboob Studio. Shammi was miffed that Goldie did not believe in close-ups. Goldie had heard that before – even Dev would insist on close-ups.

'There would be close-ups in the song, don't worry,' Goldie assured Shammi. After a few rehearsals, Shammi excused himself to the makeup room and, much to Goldie's surprise, left the studio without informing anyone. After a while Shammi returned, accompanied by Nasir Hussain. That evening, Goldie visited Hussain at his house. Hussain said, 'Shammi complains that you don't know how to shoot such a lovely song. He is worried.'

But Hussain's opinion changed when he saw the shot in the studio. He told Shammi, 'It is a wonderful shot. Don't get worried.'

Goldie was hurt that Shammi considered Hussain his guru and had complained to him rather than discussing it between them. He realized Shammi did not trust him completely, but decided not to bring up the issue with him. Goldie was clear – the day an actor did not listen to him, he would walk away from a film. He also believed that an actor would not argue for the sake of it with a talented director. And Goldie was multi-talented; he was a director, editor and an actor.

Goldie was a perennial student, wanting to learn every aspect of filmmaking. He knew he should be able to act, have a sense of music and understand lyrics; only then can he instruct actors, interact with music directors and engage with lyricists. Goldie took efforts to understand the nuances of classical music to appreciate music better.

Goldie had once heard Burman da remark about producer-director Mohan Segal, 'He has little understanding of music. How can he judge my songs?' Goldie did not want his music directors to make similar comments about him, and the only way to avoid that was to have a good knowledge about all aspects of filmmaking. A sensitive writer and director, Goldie would be in tears reading a script, often staying up nights thinking of a shot. The next morning, he would write down on a piece of paper what he had thought. If the actor did not get teary-eyed while enacting the touching scene, Goldie would blame himself for not having explained the scene properly. Unlike a poet or a painter who is solely responsible for his/her output, a film is dependent on teamwork. A good film was the result of the story writer, dialogue writer, music director, lyricist, director, producer and actors, among many others.

Goldie knew that an actor was a different animal, not inclined to listen to anyone. Their ego made them distrust the intelligence of others; it was necessary to make them feel they were right to get his work done. Goldie was aware that the director should never comment on an actor's acting skills in the presence of the crew. Whether it was Dev Anand or Amitabh Bachchan, Goldie made it a point to okay the shot and then talk to the actor in private. His gentle ways always worked. A director had to be a psychologist too.

He would act out scenes for other actors, but never for the hero. Shammi's attitude, however, made Goldie break this rule of his as he just had to show how a scene was to be enacted. This was during the shooting of the song, *Deewana mujhsa nahin*. Shammi was to walk in a swaying manner, but Goldie felt he was not in sync with the music.

'Are you now going to teach me rhythm, Goldie?' Shammi challenged.

'No! But you are not walking in rhythm.'

'I can't do better than this. The ground is uneven.'

'You are not focused. Don't be adamant. We will practise for a while with music.'

Shammi was obviously not going to take the criticism lying down. He asked Goldie to show him what he had in mind. To his surprise, Goldie did a wonderful job. He punched him jokingly, readily agreeing to the shot. Slowly but surely, they were becoming good friends.

Goldie would discuss each scene with Hussain so that he could get the script ready. Hussain, who was used to writing lengthy dialogues, respected Goldie's views and wrote accordingly. In Hussain's absence, Goldie once had to change a scene without his knowledge.

It was a romantic scene between Asha Parekh and Shammi that was to be shot before the song, *Deewana mujhsa nahin*. The scene was sent by Hussain from Mumbai, but Goldie realized that it needed to be changed. The song begins as soon as Shammi stops speaking. There was a jerkiness between the two. Shammi asked Goldie to change the dialogues, but Goldie was reluctant as he felt Hussain may not like it.

A hesitant Goldie rang up Hussain at Mumbai. He told him how he visualized the dialogues before the song: She: *Acha, ab aaiyiye, saath saath chale.*

He: *Ji nahin, hamari yahi jagah hai, peeche peeche.*

She: *Peeche peeche peeche peeche... Deeiwana toh nahin ho gaye?*

After nearly half the film was shot, it was decided to see the rushes. In Navketan no outsider, including the actors, could see the rushes. Actors had a habit of commenting on their looks and makeup after seeing the rushes. If a director changed anything based on an actor's comments, the continuity could be lost.

Seeing Shammi at the theatre, Goldie whispered,

'Why is he here?'

'He is used to seeing the rushes,' said Hussain. 'It is the industry's unwritten rule. He will object to future dates if I don't allow him here.'

Goldie decided to allow Shammi, but lost his cool when he saw Mumtaz, then famous as Dara Singh's heroine, sitting with Shammi. 'What the hell is Mumtaz doing here?' he wondered, 'She has no business to be present.' Goldie felt as if he was being stripped naked. The film is raw during rushes; no outsider had any reason to see it. Mumtaz's presence irked Goldie. He could have tolerated Shammi's wife Geeta Bali, but not Mumtaz.

An irritated Goldie refused to sit with Shammi, giving an excuse of wanting to watch the rushes carefully, without getting disturbed. Goldie decided to focus on the rushes, but was constantly disturbed by Mumtaz and Shammi chatting with each other. But soon Shammi was absorbed in the rushes. After seeing a few scenes, he jumped up to congratulate Goldie,

'I didn't feel that we were in front of the camera. Now I realize how you made us all comfortable. It's amazing!'

Goldie and Shammi's friendship deepened, and Shammi never interfered with Goldie's work again.

Whenever the shooting was at Mehboob Studio, Shammi would stay in a hotel near the studio rather than going back Pedder Road home; of course, Hussain had to bear the expenses. Each morning, Hussain would wake Shammi up, take him to Khar Gymkhana for a round of tennis, and then on to Mehboob Studio for the shooting.

One day, Shammi received a note from his then wife, Geeta Bali, that she was unwell and that he should come home immediately. He ignored it. He got another note the next morning saying she was seriously ill, but he ignored the pleas, calling it all a 'drama'. Goldie was hurt hearing Shammi talk of his wife so casually, for he respected Geeta a lot.

When he received a message the third day in a row, Shammi couldn't ignore it anymore. He rushed home to see that he had committed a grave mistake by ignoring the notes. Geeta was terribly ill, with smallpox eruptions covering her entire body. A distraut Shammi sat at her bedside till she died. Her death really shook him up.

A few days later, Hussain took Shammi to the sets of *Teesri Manzil*. 'Shammi, you take your time. I will pay the rent till you decide to come back.'

Spotting Goldie, Shammi sobbed like a child. 'I will never be able to work again, Goldie,' he repeatedly wailed.

His hands would shake so much, he was not able to even light a cigarette. He had started drinking heavily and did not shave for weeks. A few kind words and he would start crying.

'Shammi, if you don't work now, you will never be able to do so. This is the time to come out of this phase.' But Shammi was adamant. Goldie persisted, asking him to trust him. Shammi was devastated, and felt that everything was over for him.

Goldie decided to shoot one of the most difficult scenes, to challenge the actor in Shammi. Instead of breaking the scene into ten scenes, Goldie allowed the shot to remain long. It was the only way to get Shammi's confidence back. Shammi was not ready. Even the cameraman felt that it would not work, but Goldie was determined and was ready to rehearse the whole day if needed. He asked Shammi to keep his hands inside his coat pocket lest they shiver. After a couple of rehearsals, the shot was taken. Shammi was silent. It had come out well. Goldie asked for a retake. It was more to boost Shammi's confidence than for the betterment of the shot itself. As expected, Shammi performed better than the earlier one; he was back to his acting days.

Goldie was also working on *Guide* while shooting for *Teesri Manzil*. He had to ensure that the dates didn't clash. He had to go to the US for editing. He would be out for a month, he realized, and had taken care to see that the schedule of *Teesri Manzil* was not upset. Hussain had requested him to shoot the song *Dekhiye sahibon* before he left. He even offered to shoot the song in Goldie's absence, but Goldie was reluctant.

'Am I not a good director? (Subodh) Mukherjee sahab

shoots a film using four or five directors. There is a director to shoot the songs, and another for different scenes. He even uses more than a director for one song alone.'

'I understand and agree that you are a good director, but my song requires my touch. I cannot allow anyone else to do that,' Goldie said.

Hussain had raised the issue because of Shammi's dates. The set for the song was going to be expensive, costing nearly ₹5 lakhs, and he couldn't afford to lose the money due to Goldie's absence. Goldie told him, 'I will come back from the US at my own cost, but don't shoot the song. I will do it.' Hussain didn't believe Goldie, but pretended excitement. 'Wow, that's great!' he said.

Sure that Goldie would not return so quickly, he went ahead with creating the set for the song. To his surprise, Goldie returned as promised. Without saying a word, though realizing what Hussain had planned, Goldie completed the shooting.

Teesri Manzil was almost ready now.

Goldie had tried his hand at editing with *Nau Do Gyarah,* but became a full-fledged editor with *Teesri Manzil.*

A renowned editor was called in to edit *Teesri Manzil* by Hussain. Goldie did not argue. He felt that the way he had divided the shots made it easy for any editor to edit. Since he believed in detailing out his shots, his script would have notes related to long shot, close-up etc.

Goldie sat behind the editor, observing him as he began his job. When the editor was about to cut a particular frame, Goldie suggested otherwise. The man turned to look at him condescendingly, not believing a young man like Goldie could advise him! On being interrupted a second time, the editor stood up angrily. 'If you are such a good editor, why don't you do it yourself?'

'Don't get upset,' Goldie explained. 'I am the director and, hence, suggested.' But the editor was miffed. Goldie took over the task while the editor, curious to see what he does, observed him. Goldie got busy with his work, and the editor went and told Hussain, 'I don't want to work with him.'

The responsibility of editing fell on Goldie.

The initial response to the movie was lukewarm, but Goldie's work was praised. This was just when Guide was nominated for the Oscars. When Goldie returned from the US, he found out that Hussain had not screened the film beyond 21 weeks. Goldie was curious: why would Hussain, keen to see all his movies do the 'silver jubilee'. not allow this film beyond 21 weeks?

Shammi explained, 'Because he is not the director. You are. He does not want you to become a star director.'

'That's strange. After all, he is the producer, isn't he?'

Hussain was well known as a producer-director; Goldie was yet to become famous. When Goldie suggested that *Teesri Manzil* be launched as 'Vijay Anand presents', Hussain had rejected the idea.

Both *Guide* and *Teesri Manzil* started gaining popularity over time. But the accolades he got for *Guide* were far more. He had taken up the challenge to make two movies at the same time of very different genres. One was philosophical and soul-searching, while the other a murder mystery.

Goldie had turned a simple story into an extraordinary saga, and the audiences loved it. Despite having popular music, the film has stood the test of time and is watched even today.

Before *Teesri Manzil,* Shammi was known as a casual, wild dancer, but the movie gave him a very different image. There is a sense of sobriety as he goes about his antics to hide the truth from the heroine. Thanks to Goldie, Shammi comes across as a mature actor rather than someone who 'overacts.'

Keen to work with Goldie again, Shammi recommended his name to many producers, but Goldie did not work with Shammi after *Teesri Manzil.* Goldie had enjoyed making the movie, but he was wary of Shammi's 'moody' character. It was not Goldie's habit to pamper his actors. He did not want his friendship with Shammi to come in the way of his work. They remained good friends till the end.

Unwilling to pay a fixed fee, Hussain had taken on Goldie on a profit-share basis. After paying him a signing amount of

₹5,000, Hussain agreed to a 20 per cent share of the profits from Bombay territory. This was in the contract. When the contract was delivered by Hussain's brother Tahir, Goldie discovered that he would 'be given 20 per cent up to the limit of ₹50,000'.

Goldie had not expected Hussain to go back on his word! Realizing that there was no guarantee that Hussain would pay what was due even in the future, Goldie wrote on the contract, 'I don't want any share of it.'

The topic, as far as he was concerned, was closed. He never discussed it with Hussain again.

❖❖❖

While visiting the US for *Guide,* Goldie got a chance to see a film museum in New York. He realized then that he had started working on films without any formal education. Indian films had no standing among American, Russian, French and Italian cinema.

During that time, Goldie's nephew had graduated from the Film and Television Institute of India, Pune. Goldie, who had no knowledge of Swedish, Italian, French or British cinema, had heard about many international actors and directors from him.. He had never heard of François Truffaut, the famous French director, or Jean-Luc Godard, the French-Swiss film director and screenwriter. Neither of Italian director Federico Fellini and the awards he had won, nor Japanese director Akira Kurosawa whose film he saw at one of the film festivals. Goldie felt he was illiterate compared to a student from the film institute at Pune. He had self-doubts. Was he a director by chance? Was it a fluke, his success? He decided to study, to read about top directors and their works, and only then make another movie. He went to London to pursue his newfound study.

Goldie had applied to a university in London but when he reached there, they told him that there were no formal classes and that they only did research on films. They would give him a pass and he could watch as many films as he wanted.

During his 40-day stay in London, Goldie watched 60 to 70 films. He would go from one theatre to another, wanting to understand the western style of filmmaking. He watched old classics, new hits, Charlie Chaplin films, Alfred Hitchcock films, Italian films, and those by Godard, Fellini and Satyajit Ray. He watched Orson Welles' *Citizen Kane,* but he didn't like Welles' films very much. He got bored watching Michelangelo Antonioni's films and Fellini's *8½*. Goldie wondered why Fellini was considered such a great director.

However, he was impressed by the variety of subjects and the technical expertise. Goldie found the approach intellectual. The films didn't connect with the audience and didn't make them cry. The makers were using modern techniques and gimmicks. Like a Swedish filmmaker trying to show his spiritual side through a film by showing the hero playing chess with a dead man. Goldie was shocked that a lot of Londoners and critics praised the films that he himself didn't find great. Goldie was getting more and more disillusioned. Was it his incapability to make meaningful cinema preventing him from appreciating these? A strange feeling of inadequacy gripped him for a while.

Why didn't these so-called great films not affect him? He began doubting his own capabilities as a director, but then his inner voice asked, 'Do you want to make such films? Do you want to emulate others? All truly great artists carve their own niche and worked in their own way. You are unique, and you should do the same.'

Goldie finally decided that he would erase all the foreign films he had watched and also his own films from his memory and start with a clean slate. The film that appeared on his clean slate once he returned to India was *Jewel Thief.*

Goldie didn't start work on anything new until a subject inspired him so much that his heart called out from within to nudge him to do it. But Dev Anand could not lay idle for long! He liked to start on a new project as soon as the film in hand was released. *Guide* was a silver jubilee hit by now. And Dev wanted Navketan to start with its next film.

A few people in the film industry suggested to Goldie

that he should make another film like *Guide*, but he didn't want to be labelled as a particular type of director. He had seen that when an actor becomes a big star, he does the same kind of films and successful directors repeat their formula of success. Though it was a good way to succeed, Goldie found that repetitive and predictable. As the number of films Shammi Kapoor did increase in number, he became more and more 'Shammi Kapoor'. The same was the case with Raj Kapoor and Manmohan Desai. Manmohan had his typical 'lost and found' formula. In every film of his, brothers would get separated and come together. Nasir Hussain's films had a background of hotels, dances, brothers and some comedy. Goldie didn't desire to be a part of this list and wanted to create a separate niche for himself.

Goldie would forget his films once they were completed. He never watched his own films more than once. He kept a wide gap between his films, and would travel, read and write stories in that time. He would observe the events and happenings in society. He watched films of other directors and actors to get novel ideas.

Navketan was on the lookout for new subjects but Goldie couldn't think of anything new. One day Dev told him, 'There is a writer called K.A. Narayan who comes to me with new stories very often. He is quite imaginative and articulates well. You must meet him once.'

Narayan read a lot – books, newspapers, magazines and anything he could get his hands on. He had tried to make a film called *Drummer* for Filmalaya Studio. He was the writer-director of the film but after shooting five reels, Filmalaya owner Sashadhar Mukherjee threw Narayan out because he didn't like it.

Goldie liked Narayan's extroverted and talkative nature and they became good friends. Whenever they met for tea or meals, Narayan spoke and Goldie listened patiently. Narayan had narrated a few stories that Goldie found unsuitable for film. One day, as the two sat chatting, Narayan said, 'Once a policeman was interrogating a criminal. When the case goes to court, they find that the man didn't exist.'

Goldie mulled over the subject, but Narayan had told him only those two lines. *Guide* was based on spirituality, while *Kala Bazar* had a different subject. *Nau Do Gyarah* and *Tere Ghar Ke Samne* were romantic subjects. All these films had strong storylines. Goldie wanted to make a film with no story. Goldie, with his analysis and studies, had come to the conclusion that cinema should be free from other arts. He wanted cinema to stand on its own, and not compete with literature.

'Wait a minute, Narayan. I think I have found the subject for my next film. We can make a film on a man who does not exist.'

'What do you mean? What will be the story?' Narayan was dumbfounded.

'We will create a character and tell the audience that a such and such man exists. But in the end, we will show that he never actually existed. This will certainly be a challenge for the director in me.'

Narayan found Goldie's premise strange.

As they were contemplating on this storyline, Dev asked Goldie, 'Have you found a story?'

'It is the story of a jewel thief who doesn't exist. I can't tell you anything more, but I can make a fantastic film on the subject. You leave it to me.'

Dev trusted Goldie completely and so didn't ask anything further. Goldie began working on the story and screenplay. Narayan sat with him on occasions, but wasn't of too much help because he could only write stories and not visualize a film. Goldie wanted to direct a film where the storywriter wasn't noticeable. According to the real-life incident that Narayan had narrated, the police was looking for a person who didn't exist. That was the only thread Goldie had. He didn't know what transpired.

When Goldie began writing the script, he wove the story around a fictional character. When they began discussing the casting, Dev said, 'Let us think through the casting. If we take a well-known villain for the negative character, the audience will immediately guess and our story will be ruined. Who do you suggest?'

'You are the star and the producer of the film. Which popular actor do you think should work in this film?'

They first thought about Raj Kumar. Raj Kumar and Goldie were good friends once, but had not been in contact with Goldie since his 'arrest'. Dev was not keen, because of his egotistical behaviour, but it was decided to ask him once. Raj Kumar, though, did not agree after hearing the character brief from Goldie.

It was then that Goldie thought of Ashok Kumar, the veteran actor.

'I feel Dadamoni (Ashok Kumar) will be ideal for the role. He has been a hero and has done negative roles in the past. He is a born actor and doesn't get scared of any role. He was a star at one time and right now he is not as big a star as you. If he agrees to do this role, he will be very impressive as the heroine's elder brother. I think Dadamoni is great choice.'

Dev was not sure if Ashok would agree to do the role.

'Why not? His best performances have been in negative roles. *Sangram, Aarti, Gumrah, Kismet...*' Goldie said.

'Fine, let's ask him,' Dev agreed.

Ashok, who owned Bombay Talkies then, had given Dev his first break in *Ziddi*. The Anands held Ashok in high esteem. Ashok's brother Kishore Kumar, too, had started his playback singing career with his first song for Dev in *Ziddi*.

Dev called Ashok's secretary only to find out that he had just returned from America and not taking too much work. 'He is at Rooptara Studio at Dadar. Come at lunchtime,' the secretary said.

When they reached the studio, Ashok was having lunch in a small air-conditioned makeup room, with a bib around his neck to protect his clothes.

He welcomed them warmly and Dev told him about the new movie being made by Goldie.

'People are praising you a lot, and say there will not be a director like Goldie again,' Ashok said, looking at Goldie.

'If that is the case, will you work with me?'

Dadamoni asked Goldie with a chuckle, 'Have you ever asked me to work with you?'

'I am asking you now.'

'Fine with me. What is your proposal?

'Dadamoni, films are made for Dev Papa at Navketan. In this movie, *Jewel Thief,* we want you to do the title role. I am not able to think of anyone other than you. I must tell you about the twist in the film where the Jewel Thief turns out to be the villain in the end. You have played negative characters before and I am sure you will do this role really well. For this role, I want an actor whose image is larger than Dev Anand. I have nothing more to add. I will narrate the story to you some time later.'

Ashok laughed aloud and said, 'I will certainly do the film. Goldie, I love Dev and you. I have heard so much about you that I, too, want to work with you. I don't care whether this is a negative or any other kind of role.' He paused for a while before continuing, 'You are aware that I have just got my bypass surgery done. I hope you won't kill me at the end of the film?' He chuckled at his own joke.

'I will neither kill you, nor allow you to be abused. There is no violence or action in this film. The climax is truly befitting you.'

'I hope I, too, am not expected to kill anyone? Does it require me to do physical violence?' Ashok raised another doubt.

'No... Not at all.'

'I don't mind running to a car to escape or something like that,' Ashok added.

He looked at Dev. 'Please speak with my secretary regarding the dates.'

The brothers were elated at Ashok Kumar's acceptance. As they were leaving, Ashok said to Goldie, 'I have still not completely recovered from my surgery. Firstly, I will not be able to come to the sets before 11 in the morning, and secondly, the doctor has asked me to have lunch exactly 1.30. And finally, I will not shoot after 5 in the evening. I can work for five hours – 11 to 1 and then 2 to 5. Please remember these three conditions.'

Goldie nodded in acknowledgement. He was fine with all the conditions.

'Anything else...?' Dev hesitated, hinting at the payment Ashok would expect.

'You may speak to my secretary about that too.'

It was now the turn to choose the heroine. Vyjayanthimala was the first name that cropped up because there was an important dance sequence in the film and she was a fantastic dancer. Goldie had watched her films but never worked with her. He had heard that she was a little temperamental, but he decided to give it a shot.

Goldie fixed up a meeting with her and went to her house. Dr. Bali was also present. Dr. Bali and Vyjayanthimala were in a relationship, but Goldie didn't know much about it. Dr. Bali's wife, Ruby, was Nargis' cousin and a frequent visitor to the Anand household. Formal talks between Goldie and Vyjayanthimala began, but he was hesitant to narrate the story in Dr. Bali's presence. He just wouldn't leave! Vyjayanthimala asked, 'Can we start?'

Goldie just glanced at Dr. Bali without saying a word. He couldn't openly say that he didn't want to narrate the story with him around. Dr. Bali got the hint, but he said, 'I listen to all the scripts.'

Goldie found this strange, and wondered if he had come to the right place and person. He had no choice and started narrating the story, but he didn't look at Dr. Bali even once during his narration. He was least bothered about Dr. Bali's reaction or whether he liked the story. Goldie narrated his story for almost one and a half hours with all the minute details. After he finished, Vyjayanthimala asked, 'But who is the jewel thief?'

Goldie was stunned and Dr. Bali laughed. It meant that she was not very sharp and had not grasped the story. Dr. Bali said, turning towards her, 'Didn't you get it? The whole Ramayana is over and you ask who Ram is?'

Then he told Goldie, 'Excellent! This is a unique and beautiful story.'

It was then that Goldie realized that Dr. Bali's presence was a blessing in disguise. As he had approved of the story, Vyjayanthimala agreed to do the film immediately.

Tanuja was chosen for a short but important role. Shobhna Samarth felt that associating with Goldie would help Tanuja's career. Seeing Tanuja's vibrant and impish personality, Goldie thought she would be ideal for the part. Tanuja was fit for Anju's mischievous, restless and innocent character. Anju Mahendru, Nazir Hussain (character actor) and others were chosen for different roles.

Dev was away shooting in Copenhagen. Goldie called him and asked him to buy a smart cap from there. Goldie wanted Amar's character in the film to wear a cap because he was a glamorous and suspicious character. Dev, anyway loved wearing caps and hats in his films. The cap Dev bought from Copenhagen went on to become a highlight of the film.

After doing the music for *Hum Dono,* music director Jaidev wanted to make a place for himself in Navketan, but that was impossible till S.D. Burman was around. Jaidev hoped that he would be asked to do the music for *Jewel Thief* and he expressed his desire to the Anand brothers. But Goldie felt that Sachin da would be a better choice; he did the music eventually. Shailendra was chosen to write the songs. The three of them had a fantastic tuning and they constantly sat together and worked on the music.

When Shailendra wrote the song, *Rula ke gaya sapna mera, baithee hoon kab ho savera,* Goldie asked, 'Can you use *mera* instead of *tera*? (the word suggested earlier was *tera*). It is her dream but it has a double meaning. When the audience watches the film the second time, they will realize that the heroine is truly sad; at the same time, she is also acting sad deliberately. She is trying to tell the hero that she is madly in love with him and the word *mera* would be apt. But the audience will realize that what she is saying is not true.'

Shailendra was convinced by Goldie's explanation and changed the word.

Shailendra was writing *Hothon pe aisi baat* next. The tune was ready and the introductory lines were in place, but he was stuck. Goldie would give Shailendra a deadline but he never met it. Finally, Goldie went to Shailendra's house.

'He is not at home.' That was the answer Goldie got from inside the house. Goldie waited for two days and went again. Goldie realized that Shailendra was avoiding him. Later, Goldie got to know that there was a problem with the film *Teesri Kasam* that Shailendra was producing. Raj Kapoor, the hero of the film, was not giving the dates. One day Goldie caught Shailendra at home. Shailendra was very distressed and anxious. He had started drinking a lot too. He had taken loans for his film and the shooting was stuck. Shailendra promised that he would write the song soon, but it was the same story again. Shailendra avoided meeting Goldie. Finally, Goldie wrote a letter to Shailendra, saying, 'Only your close friends can help you. Isolating yourself, not meeting people or drinking is not the solution.'

He didn't receive any response from Shailendra and soon learnt about Shailendra's death. Majrooh Sultanpuri was requested to write the lyrics. Goldie considered Majrooh a great poet and thought that he wrote beautiful, touching songs.

Shooting started and the first scene was shot at Mehboob Studio. The set was that of character actor Sapru's house. Goldie set up the lighting and got the technical rehearsals done between 9 and 11 in the morning. Ashok Kumar was supposed to reach the set with his makeup done at 11, as decided earlier. Goldie ensured that all the actors in the film were present on the first day of the shoot and participated in the shooting. Goldie knew that if actors are made to sit the whole day without any shooting, they feel neglected and don't work wholeheartedly.

Dev Anand, Ashok Kumar, Vyjayanthimala, Sapru, Tanuja and all the other actors were in the first scene. It was the scene of Tanuja's birthday party shot at her house. This was where Vyjayanthimala and Ashok see Dev for the first time and address him as 'Amar'. Dev replies he is not Amar and that his name is Vinay. There is an argument between the three. Ashok asks Dev to show his feet, as Amar had six toes. When Dev shows his feet with five toes, Ashok is stunned.

Ashok reached the set sharp at 11. Both Ashok and Dev memorized their lines while Vyjayanthimala got her makeup done. Goldie had informed her that Ashok would be punctual.

The shot was ready. Goldie asked his assistant to bring Vyjayanthimala to the set.

'She said she is coming.'

Time passed and it was almost 12 noon. Every time the assistant went to her makeup room and told her that the shot was ready and that everyone was waiting for her, she would just say, 'I am coming'.

After some time, she locked her makeup room door from inside. Her assistant, who stood at the door, did not allow Goldie's assistant inside. It was half past 12 now.

'Tell them I am coming,' she shouted from inside.

Goldie didn't know what to do. He thought he had made a big mistake signing Vyjayanthimala. Nothing could be done now. He sat cursing himself.

Ten minutes before 1, she stepped out with her anklets tinkling, with her makeup man, hairdresser and dress man in tow.

There was no point rehearsing any more as they had to break for lunch exactly at 1 for Dadamoni. Goldie was furious. He had a lot of respect for Ashok and had promised him that his schedule will be taken care of.

'Mr. Vijay Anand, what do I have to do?'

Goldie was livid at Vyjayanthimala's question.

She had the audacity to be late, didn't feel any remorse and didn't have a word of apology!

'We're breaking for lunch,' he curtly told her.

'What is this? You have been calling me to the sets for so long and now when I come ready for the shot, you declare a lunch break?' she snapped.

'Listen,Vyjayanthi! I had informed you earlier that the doctors have asked Dadamoni to eat at 1 o'clock sharp and if his lunch is delayed, he will have acidity and fall ill. You came to the set at ten minutes to 1. We could have shot the scene if you had come by 12. It is better you go for lunch now and come to the set at 2. We will rehearse once and then shoot the scene. And, yes, please don't be late to the sets tomorrow onwards. Eleven means eleven! If you want to come at twelve forty-five, please inform me in advance so that I will not fix your shot before that,' Goldie said firmly.

Vyjayanthimala was a big star and the other producer-directors danced to her tune. She didn't like Goldie's tone and went back to her makeup room in a huff.

Ashok tried to cool tempers down. 'Goldie, it's okay if it's a few minutes here and there.'

'Goldie, don't spoil your relationship with Vyjayanthimala on the first day itself,' cameraman Virendra Ratra advised.

'He is the director and I think what he did was right.' Dev came to Goldie's support.

'I don't want to make a film in this manner. If Vyjayanthimala wants to work with me, she better come to the set on time.'

Everyone dispersed for lunch and the issue was closed.

Goldie, Dev and Ashok were back on set sharp at 2. Vyjayanthimala was annoyed and came fifteen minutes late. Goldie didn't say anything. They did one rehearsal and he took the shot. Vyjayanthimala was behaving as if nothing had happened. Perhaps she was feeling guilty. If it hadn't been a star as big as Ashok Kumar, she would have surely left the sets.

In a way, her anger turned out to be beneficial for Goldie because she had to act as if she was angry in the scene to be shot!

Goldie realized after two to three days of the shooting that whenever Dr. Bali was present on the sets, Vyjayanthimala would not come out for hours. The first thing Goldie asked his assistant on arriving on the set was, 'Has Dr. Bali come? Then let us not have the first shot with Vyjayanthimala.' Dr. Bali would ignore Goldie and walk straight into Vyjayanthimala's makeup room. Goldie found Dr. Bali's behaviour strange and rude. Dr. Bali could never have good relations with Goldie because Ruby's family was very close to the Anands. Dr. Bali would get Vyjayanthimala's lunch, and once he entered her make room, the door would remain shut.

Producers and directors didn't find it odd if the husbands of actresses came to the sets, but Dr. Bali was not married to Vyjayanthimala then. Dr. Bali would raise his eyebrows or make a face whenever they were shooting a romantic scene. Dev and Vyjayanthimala found it difficult to do such scenes with ease in his presence. Goldie had to explain every scene to her in detail. 'See, you have to walk from here, stop there and then give him a loving look...' and so on.

Once she understood the scene, Vyjayanthimala would do a fantastic job, but if Goldie read the screenplay to explain the scene she would get confused. Goldie had understood how to elicit work out of her. He realized that he shouldn't tax her brains too much. Goldie, anyway, had never considered her a great actress. Goldie felt that the chemistry between Dev and Vyjayanthimala never got established because she had been arrogant to him a few times. In one of the scenes, they had to go down to the cellar and hug each other. She insisted that the camera focus only on her face in the scene. Since they were supposed to be meeting after a long time, Dev felt the expressions of both should be shown.

'Why are you objecting?' asked Dev.

'This is my shot,' she said.

'I am there too. Let me enact my way and you do yours.'

There would be arguments over such trivial matters. The two had acted in other films together before *Jewel Thief*, but there was no camaraderie between them.

Vyjayanthimala was chosen for the film for her excellent dancing skills; and yet it was important to get her to rehearse for the song, *Hothon pe aisi baat*. Dance masters Hiralal and Sohanlal gave her a lot of respect and addressed her as 'Amma'. Goldie had told the duo that the song will have very lengthy shots and if she didn't rehearse they would have to take several retakes. It would be a problem if she forgot the steps during the shoot. They should ensure that she practices for a day, he told them.

They asked Vyjayanthimala to rehearse. She said, 'That is okay. We will rehearse a day before the shoot.' However, she did not turn up for the rehearsal as promised. When she came for the shoot the next day, Goldie told her, 'Vyjayanthi, this is a difficult song.'

'Nothing difficult... What is there in it? You don't worry. I will do my makeup and come to the set.'

'No! You rehearse today. I will cancel the shooting for the day. Since I have paid the rent for the day, you can rehearse here itself.'

'Why should you cancel the shooting? I will do the scene well.'

'It's not about doing well or not. You are no doubt a brilliant dancer, but it is important to rehearse for this song. I want this to be one of your most memorable dances. I don't think you should feel inferior rehearsing for the song.'

Sohanlal said to Goldie, 'You go home. I will get her to practice.'

Goldie left and as soon as he reached home, he received a call from the studio, saying Vyjayanthimala had left. 'Amma said she will rehearse at home,' Hiralal said.

Saroj Khan, who later became a renowned choreographer, was Hiralal-Sohanlal's assistant, and the duo had sent her to Vyjayanthi's house for rehearsal. When Goldie asked Saroj Khan if Vyjayanthi had rehearsed, she replied that she only did the hand movements.

'Did she do any of the twirls and gyrations?' Goldie asked worriedly.

'Yes, she did a few.'

Goldie wondered how the shoot would be the next day. To Goldie's surprise, it went very well. Vyjayanthimala was undoubtedly a brilliant and natural dancer. People remember her mesmerizing dance in the song even today. In Goldie's opinion, had she rehearsed more sincerely, she would have done even better. Goldie realized that at times he expected too much from the actors. Actors were not always wrong. Goldie had expected Vyjayanthi to practice as hard as Waheeda had done for *Guide*. This was an unfair comparison because Vyjayanthi was a consummate dancer and did not need so much practice.

But the incident left a bad taste in his mouth and Goldie didn't enjoy working with Vyjayanthimala. Her attitude was cold and she behaved as if she was obliging him by coming to the set. She never discussed anything much about the scenes with Goldie and neither was there a nod of satisfaction on giving a good shot. On the other hand, Goldie was proud that he had a wonderful understanding with Ashok Kumar.

A big portion of the film was shot in Sikkim – this being the first time a film was shot there. There were no proper roads or buses there. The day the unit reached, there was a massive hailstorm there. Goldie, Dev and Ashok were jumping around like children seeing the hailstorm. Ashok was so excited seeing the rock-like hailstones and the loud clatter they made that he ran around collecting them. He told the cameraman, Virendra, to take out his camera and shoot the storm.

Since there was no electricity, Virendra could not capture that beautiful sight. Goldie had chosen Sikkim because the script required it. He wanted a place that was a part of India, yet felt foreign. Goldie didn't want to go to Nepal because it wasn't a part of India. When Dev and Goldie went to Sikkim to check out the location, they met King Chogyal and became very good friends with him. Army General Bhagat Singh was very impressed with the Anand brothers, and as there were no bus services available, offered them the use of army unit jeeps.

As promised, Bhagat Singh's platoon helped the unit a lot

with the shooting. The local army officers would host parties for the film unit every evening, and demanded that the young women in the uniit go with them for these parties. It became difficult for Goldie and Dev to manage the situation because the army officers would insist on taking the girls with them.

One day, an army officer told Goldie, 'We would like to take Anju Mahendru to a party with us tonight.

'No, you can't do that. She has an early morning shoot and needs to retire early. As a rule, no one in our unit is allowed to go out alone. If you really insist, all of us will come along, too.'

Anju's mother had accompanied her to Sikkim, and she stressed at way the officer was insistent. Goldie said, 'If you want to take Anju with you, her mother and some unit members will also accompany her.' That apparently cooled tempers off.

When the unit was on outdoor shoots, everyone had fun, but even there, Vyjayanthi didn't mix too much and kept to herself. The only thing she was worried about was being able to make phone calls. The moment she got some free time, she would run to book trunk calls to Bombay. The phone lines were not very clear and she had to speak very loudly on the phone. Her voice would be audible to the whole unit and they would know who she was talking to and what she was saying.

Goldie knew a lot was happening in her life but he found her behaviour weird. He just couldn't gel with her the way he had hoped. Luckily, her role was not very important in the film. It was Ashok Kumar who had the key role to play, apart from Goldie as the director. Dev Anand's character was central to the plot, while Vaijayanthimala's role didn't stand out as much. Her lacklustre performance worked in the film's favour because if she had done very well it would have, in some sense, ruined the balance of the film. Vyjayanthi's performance was just adequate and she was neither praised nor criticized by the viewers.

Contrary to Vyjayanthimala's serious demeanour, it was Tanuja who would lighten the mood. Goldie and Tanuja became very close during the shoot. She played around so much that it was sometimes difficult to control her. She would tease everyone, pull the cameraman's ears and create havoc on the sets. Sometimes she would pick up a cushion from the props and throw it at Goldie. Tanuja's mother Shobhna Samarth would tell Goldie, 'You are the only one who can control my daughter.'

Whenever it was Tanuja's shot, Goldie would tell her, 'Tanu, for God's sake, sit here quietly, otherwise I will tie you up.'

He had to treat her like a child. She would lean on Goldie's shoulder, pull his ears or his cheeks, and yet he loved working with her. He used her mischievous nature to the full for Anju's character in the film.

Goldie wanted to cast Tanuja in an important role in his forthcoming film, but a reputed producer-director from the South loved Tanuja's performance in *Jewel Thief* so much that he signed her as the heroine in his film *Jeene Ki Raah*. The success of that film made Tanuja a big star and her career took roots. Goldie found Tanuja to be very energetic, enthusiastic and full of wild passion for her work. She had a beautiful face with a dazzling smile, but her profile was flawed. Goldie felt that if one could channelize her exuberance and youth, Tanuja could an extraordinary actress. She gave her all for the song, *Raat akeli hai*.

The relationship between the Anand brothers and Vyjayanthimala soured so much during the making of *Jewel Thief* that she didn't even come for the film's trial show. They didn't meet each other once the film was released.

Despite that Goldie regretted never working with her again. Goldie had very cordial and friendly relationships with all his heroines, be it Nanda, Sadhana, Tanuja, Nutan, Waheeda or Mumtaz.

Immediately after the completion of *Jewel Thief*, Dr. Bali got divorced from his first wife Ruby and got married to Vyjayanthimala. The Anand family was very unhappy with his divorce from Ruby.

The bitterness Vyjayanthimala had for Goldie remained

for a long time. A few years ago, when she was conferred with the Padmashri, Goldie was in England. He sent her a congratulatory telegram, reminiscing about the times they had worked together.

In her reply to Goldie, Vyjayanthi had written, 'You may think you are intelligent, but we don't care about you.'

Goldie was quite certain that the letter must have been written by Dr. Bali and not Vyjayathimala because he did not think her capable of such fluent English!

Jewel Thief got released with Ashok Kumar's name featuring right on top in the credits. Goldie had asked Dev if they could present the title as 'Dev Anand presents Ashok Kumar in *Jewel Thief*'? Dev agreed to his name featuring after Ashok in the credits.

The film didn't get a positive response immediately. But it improved over time. Other than *Johny Mera Naam,* none of Goldie's movies had received success on the day of the launch. But Goldie never chased commercial success. He was not after money; he was happy and proud that his films were remembered more than thirty years after they were released.

❖❖❖

Producer Gulshan Rai, having distributed *Guide* and *Jewel Thief,* had developed close relations with the Anands. When he produced a movie that did no fared well, his friend, B.R. Chopra, advised him to stick to film distribution. Rai promised himself that he would make a hit movie one day and show the world! Rai used to visit Hoshiarpur often. There were many astrologers in Hoshiarpur who followed the Maharishi Bhrigu tradition of horoscopes. When Rai asked about his future, he was told that a person called Goldie would make his film successful. (Rai had a lot of faith in Maharishi Bhrigu and would have his image shown before the Trimurti Films logo). Rai had no doubts about Goldie's capabilities. Another astrologer, Maula sahib who worked with producer Madan Mohla, too had asked him to take Goldie's help. Maula sahab was very popular and many directors, producers and actors used to take his advice.

Rai requested Goldie to work on a film produced by him. Dev Anand was in favour of the idea, too, and was agreeable to the movie being made outside the Navketan banner.

When Goldie demanded ₹5 lakhs for the film, Rai countered by offering him one-third partnership in the production. 'You are like a brother to me,' he said. Goldie, sentimental at heart, could not refuse, and agreed to the partnership. He took a token amount of ₹5,000.

Rai wanted to make a movie based on a story written by K.A. Narayan, who had written *Jewel Thief*. Goldie was fine with the suggestion, though he knew that Narayan did not have much idea of a screenplay.

'I will work on the story once we select it. Leave the rest to me,' Goldie told Rai. Rai suggested that they take Kalyanji-Anandji as music directors, and wanted to include a tune he liked. Goldie was clear. 'I will use the song only if it suits the scene. Otherwise, I am fine to work with whomsoever you decide. You are the producer.'

Goldie's self-confidence allowed him to work with any actor, music director, writer or lyricist. He started working on the script. The story as narrated by Narayan was flat. It was about two brothers getting separated when young. One of the brothers goes astray and later whips his mother. Goldie was not agreeable to showing a son hitting his mother, and decided to change the script to make it more appealing. He developed other characters while working on the story and the script.

Rai was clear about his objective. 'I am not bothered about the story. All I want is to make a commercial film which will mint money. I have put all my money into it and I want to prove to B.R. Chopra and others that I can make a hit film.'

Goldie assured Rai that he knew the formula for success. The film was to be titled *Do Roop* but Rai, a believer in numerology and astrology, wanted a 'lucky' name and was told that the movie should start with 'J'. And that's how *Johny Mera Naam* happened.

Rai introduced Goldie to a new actress, Hema Malini, who had just started working on a film, *Sapno Ka Saudagar.* Goldie saw the trials and was not impressed. He did not like her South Indian accent, her walking style, and that she was a little plump, like many heroines from the South.

Rai insisted that Goldie meet her once before deciding to reject her. As expected, Goldie's views changed. She was better-looking in person. Goldie noticed that she was self-assured and her eyes were bright. The only flaw, if at all, was that she was not western-looking like Goldie wanted for *Johny Mera Naam*. Goldie decided to show the transformation of a typical Indian girl into one who gets into smuggling. This was part of the screenplay and Goldie was confident he could show the transformation with Hema Malini.

He then went about selecting her clothes and deciding a hairstyle to suit her broad forehead. Initially, Hema Malini did not like the selection of clothes but Goldie convinced her.

Goldie was keen to take Premnath as the villain. He was a good friend and his acting was loud, which suited the role Goldie had in mind. Premnath had failed to make an impression in *Teesri Manzil*. So Goldie wanted to give him another chance to get his popularity back.

Goldie called Premnath to the sets. 'I will come to meet you but not to discuss anything about the movie,' Premnath insisted.

On the third call, Premnath agreed to meet Goldie. When Goldie reached his home at Chembur, he found Premnath watching one of his own old movies along with friends and actress Kamini Kaushal. He was also enjoying some recreational drugs while watching, and would jump up with joy whenever his wife Bina Rai came on the screen. He would go and kiss her on the 16-mm screen.

When Goldie mentioned the role in his upcoming film, Premnath bluntly refused, saying he was not interested. Goldie was dejected. He said, 'If I knew you would refuse, I would not have the proposed character in the script itself.'

Premnath used to meet ascetics and astrologers. He remembered meeting an ascetic from the Himalayas who had told him that a role would be proposed to him and that he should not refuse, because it would get him his stardom back. Recalling the incident, Premnath immediately agreed to the role.

Goldie had seen the way Premnath behaved at home; that gave him the inspiration for the character in the movie. Apart from the hero, the hero's brother had an important role in the movie. Those days Pran was known for enacting character and villain roles. The role of the hero's brother, while it starts off as a negative one, turns positive, and Goldie chose Pran for it. Normally, Dev Anand would speak to those who were selected for a role, and Goldie did not have to bother about casting. But he decided to meet Pran. After all, he was a highly rated actor and producers would be queuing up to meet him.

Goldie was not sure if Pran would agree, given his extremely busy schedule. But Gulshan Rai suggested that it would be good for Pran's ego if Goldie personally met him. He was received warmly by Pran, who hugged him. While having a cup of tea, Goldie broached the topic of his movie. In response, Pran took out his diary and said, 'Here! Look at my dates. If you can find some vacant slots, I am all yours.'

Goldie realized that it was Pran's way of politely refusing his offer.

Pran was surprised at Goldie's reaction, or rather lack of it. He told his secretary after Goldie left, 'For the first time I am seeing a man who did not insist on my dates. He never tried to pamper my ego. Is it arrogance or self-confidence? I am impressed by this man. We need to find the dates. I want to work in the film.'

Goldie was wondering whom he should approach for the role now when he got a call from Pran confirming his availability!

Padma Khanna, a struggling dancer, came to meet Goldie. She was not at her best when she met Goldie; teeth red with chewing paan, nails cut haphazardly, a sweaty face. She was attractive though. Goldie believed in giving new actors a chance to prove themselves. He knew they would put in their best and not throw 'star tantrums'. There was a character in the script who works with the villain only to run away with all his money. The character had a glamorous girlfriend who was a dancer. When he gets caught, the girlfriend, using her charm and dancing, tries to save her lover. Padma Khanna was a kathak dancer. Goldie told her, 'I will give you the role but you will have to work hard. Firstly, you need to see a dentist. Don't mind me being blunt, but you need to take care of your teeth. I will pay the dentist's fees.'

He continued, 'Start wearing western clothes. I will send a dance master who will teach you western dance styles. Forget kathak for a while.'

Padma Khanna merely nodded in agreement. She followed whatever Goldie had advised, including the dental treatment. Dance master Suresh taught her the steps.

The famous comedian, I.S. Johar, played the role of three identical brothers. This was the first time a person was doing three roles.

It was a movie where each actor fit a role to a T, be it the hero's father or the temple priest who steals the idols from the temple. While Goldie was busy with the casting, the music duo of Kalyanji-Anandji was perfecting the tunes. Goldie and they had become good friends within a short time. Kalyanji was interested in horse racing and would invite Goldie to the race course. They would often meet at home and enjoy a round of pani puri.

While Goldie enjoyed the social meetings, work was getting delayed. When Goldie expressed his concern, the duo said, 'Don't worry, that will be done.'

Goldie was not very impressed with the song *Nafrat karne walon ke,* but he agreed as Gulshan Rai really loved the line,

'Main woh parvana hoon jo pathar ko mom kar doon'. Kalyanji-Anandji always had a repertoire of tunes ready with them, and were, therefore, able to do their job fast. Goldie realized pretty soon that it was worthwhile to sit with Anandji for the tunes rather than Kalyanji. Anandji was good at creating tunes for a serious song, one that touched the heart, while Kalyanji had the pulse on what would sell. But Goldie did not chase popularity for the sake of it; he was more concerned with a unique tune rather than the success of a song.

Anandji would be busy the whole day in the recording room for the background music, making it difficult for Goldie to spend time with him. Kalyanji liked to spend the evening playing cards. Goldie worked with Anandji on songs like *O babul pyare* and *Pal bhar ke liye.*

But the tunes needed elder brother Kalyanji's approval. 'While we were chatting last evening, we came up with these tunes. Do you want to listen?' Goldie would suggest.

Kalyanji, knowing Goldie's ploy and the fact that he liked to work with Anandji, would give his assent. Kalyanji knew that Anandji was doing a fantastic job and so did not object to his tunes being chosen.

Goldie admired lyricist Rajendra Krishan, especially his lack of arrogance or ego. He had a great sense of humour too. Those days he was working for films being made in the South. He was also a dialogue writer. He would suggest, 'Don't go for too heavy or too gaudy. Let it be light!'

The movie was almost ready but the music duo was yet to perfect the tune for the *Husn ke lakhon rang* song. It took them nearly twenty days to get it right. This is the song where a woman (Padma Khanna) does everything to try and save her lover, who had cheated his boss, the villain (Premnath). She is desperate to tempt the boss so that he would fall for her and she is willing to go to any level to make it happen. Finally, she manages to lure him. She challenges him in the song to try and touch her.

Goldie wanted the song to have an S.D. Burman feel, with

its sensual, flowing beat but Kalyanji-Anandji were unable to get the same. Goldie asked them to focus on the rhythm first. The music duo's younger brother Babla was a rhythm master. Goldie asked them to break down the words. The word *dekhoge* was broken into *dekho...ge*!

Goldie gave the example of how S.D. Burman used to break words. In a song from the movie *Jewel Thief*, for example, the words are

Raat akeli hai
bujh gaye diye
aa ke mere paas
kano mein mere
jo bhi chahe kahiye...

It was a challenge for Kalyanji-Anandji, one they took head on. With the music duo working together with the director and the lyricist, they finally got it right!

While shooting, Hema Malini did not enjoy the rehearsals and would be keen on the final takes. Her self-confidence prevented her from putting in her best in the rehearsals. But she was a good listener and a learner, though she tired quickly. She would, while shooting a song sequence, hum the words to herself. She was used to lip movement thanks to her dance performances on stage.

Goldie had a way of getting the best out of his actors without making them realize that they had worked so hard. Unfortunately, or maybe because of the hard work Goldie made her do, Hema Malini never mentions him as one of her top directors. *Johny Mera Naam* was a turning point for Hema Malini, catapulting her into stardom. Goldie and she were good friends. Their relationship was platonic and Hema Malini's mother, Jaya Chakravarthy, did not mind Goldie visiting their house to discuss the scenes.

Johny Mera Naam was a challenging project for Goldie who had never made an out an out commercial film. Luckily, producer Gulshan Rai treated him like a younger brother and had given him complete freedom, be it casting or in money matters, including selection of location, hotel and other things.

Rai had burnt his fingers in earlier films and was desperate to see success. Goldie realized the burden he had on his shoulders and put in extra efforts. Rai rarely visited the sets, simply enquiring on the phone. When asked why he does not visit the sets, he would answer, 'Goldie is the producer, not me.'

Hema Malini was not happy with the hotel room in Kathmandu. Her brother, who had accompanied her, wanted a separate room. Goldie solved the problem by vacating his room and booking himself in a smaller hotel nearby. He used to behave like a producer, conscious of the money being spent. Rai was surprised that Goldie had not asked him for money despite working so hard. He asked him once, 'Goldie, how come you have not demanded money yet?'

'I will take it when you earn enough. I don't need money right now,' Goldie assured him.

Rai was thrilled with Goldie's response and wanted him to become a third partner but Goldie refused, saying he will think about it. 'First you get your debts cleared,' Goldie advised Rai.

The set for a temple had been erected in Mumbai for the *O babul pyare* song, but Hema Malini refused to come as she had not been paid her dues. Dev Anand and Pran were ready with their makeup but Hema Malini did not turn up despite sending reminders. When Pran suggested packing up for the day, Goldie said, 'I will shoot your scenes.'

'How is that possible? My shots are with Dev and Hema, aren't they?'

'I have changed the shot division and can complete the scenes in just a few hours. Don't worry.'

Pran was surprised at the way Goldie kept costs in mind. He promised Goldie that if he were to become a producer someday, he would hire him for the job.

The movie was more than half ready. The song *Pal bhar ke liye koi hame pyar kar le* was to be shot. Goldie had created a specially designed glass house for it. The scene shows Dev and Hema Malini arguing as Dev did not meet her father as promised. Their romance, Hema's mock anger, the way she pushes Dev out of the house... all lead to the song.

Goldie was clear on how Dev would enact the song; he designed the windows to open in one direction. He knew that Dev was not a dancer like Jeetendra or a serious actor like Raj Kapoor.

While shooting the song *Husn ke lakhon rang*, he had instructed dance master Suresh to teach Padma Khanna western moves. She was not used to it and her steps would resemble a mujra during practice. Suresh and Padma worked hard and the final take was much to Goldie's satisfaction. Her dance and Premnath's reaction to it left everyone impressed. So real were his expressions, that at times Goldie worried that Premnath might hug Padma Khanna out of sheer lust!

It was time to shoot the climax: Dev and Pran are fighting with each other when they realize they are brothers separated in childhood. They decide to confront the villain but their mother gets kidnapped. In the scene where the brothers confront the villain, it is Pran who saves their mother. He was a negative character earlier but comes to the rescue in the end.

People were surprised that Goldie had not made Dev the hero in the end. Even Dev was not exactly happy at the way Goldie had visualized the scene. For Goldie, every person who came before the camera was the hero at that moment. He did not differentiate between a star and other actors. But the ego of the stars prevented many directors from taking such an approach.

Goldie had to face the censor board once again. They had objections to the song, *Husn ke lakhon rang*, terming it lewd and too bold for the viewers. Goldie tried explaining the scene. He also defended the scene, saying that the villain never touches the dancer even once. He had over-dressed Padma, and while she achieved the desired effect as she removed some of her clothes, she still does not look 'cheap'. 'Her partial nudity is more attractive than nudity itself,' he justified.

After a lot of debate, the censor board agreed to clear the song. When one sees the kind of lewd songs shown in movies today, that song in *Johny Mera Naam* looks decent!

Dev's career was not exactly rocking while shooting *Johny Mera Naam,* though Hema Malini's *Sapno Ka Saudagar* was a hit. Goldie was not sure how the viewers would react to the movie. It is a different matter that Premnath as a villain became really popular and started a new journey. The movie became a launch pad for Pran and Kalyanji-Anandji.

Johny Mera Naam was declared a hit in the very first week. The other movies released then were Dilip Kumar's *Gopi* and Raj Kapoor's *Mera Naam Joker.* But *Johny Mera Naam* beat all of them. The commercial formula had worked!

Goldie shines as a dialogue writer in the movie. The dialogues for Dev Anand are especially enjoyable. With Dev's inimitable style and the long dialogues that suited him, his lines make a tremendous impact. In Goldie's films songs emerge from the dialogues. In the song, *Nafrat karne walon ke,* for example, the heroine asks Dev Anand what he was seeing.

He wonders why the sun and moon are in the sky at the same time, referring to her eyes.

Upset by his blatant flirting, she says she hates such things. The song begins then.

The song *Chhup chhup Meera roye* is placed appropriately and evokes the emotions of the scene very well. The character, Rekha, has been asked to steal jewels from a temple, and she is filled with guilt. In the earlier scenes we see a young girl being kidnapped, so viewers are already tense. When Rekha puts her hand out to steal the jewels, she hesitates, withdrawing her hand as if stung by a snake. Goldie finds it a magical moment to introduce the song. A girl drawn into smuggling as she searches for her lost father and her internal fight, her angst while trying to steal the temple jewelry, it is all captured beautifully through the song:

Chhup chhup Meera roye
dard na jaane koi...

After an intense exchange of dialogues between Bhupendra Singh and Ranjit, characters in the movie, the song *O babul pyare* shows us the emotions Bhupendra Singh is experiencing. The words express the anguish and its intensity. It is an audio-visual treat.

Goldie could add Urdu words to the dialogues with ease. Even a viewer who did not understand Urdu would get the meaning listening to the full dialogue.

The movie was a hit and Goldie was sure that, despite no written agreement, Gulshan Rai would stick to his promise of giving him a third of the share. But Rai only asked, 'Goldie, state your price?' He seemed to have forgotten his promise. Goldie was stumped. The man who had promised a share was now talking of a fee! Gulshan placed ₹1lakh on the table. Goldie had treated Rai like an elder brother, and was shocked at the change of behaviour. He said, returning the money, 'I don't want any money.'

Rai didn't say anything and left quietly. Goldie sat stunned. How could a man go back on his word after the movie was a super-hit? Rai pleaded with Dev too. He had to pay Dev ₹12lakhs for the film but he pleaded his inability, stating lack of distributor support. Dev asked, 'What do you want me to do?'

'If you can take ₹2 lakhs less,' Gulshan Rai begged. Goldie had been sitting in the same room. Dev said, 'I am fine to let go off the amount now but if the movie does well, you will pay me the balance.' Rai agreed, but when *Johny Mera Naam* succeeded at the box office, he did not keep his promise.

Initially, the movie was screened with the words 'Vijay Anand presents', but later, after a year or so, when the new prints were released, the words were 'Gulshan Rai's *Johny Mera Naam*'. Goldie, as per his nature, didn't argue or raise the issue with the producer.

Rai presumed Goldie would be willing to direct his next movie too. He met Dev in that regard, but Goldie flatly refused, saying, 'I don't want to do anything with you.'

'Did I do anything wrong?' Rai asked, putting on an innocent face.

Goldie did not answer. Rai begged Dev to intervene and Dev did try to convince Goldie. 'I don't have anything against him but I will not work with him in the future,' said Goldie. He was clear about what he would not do.

Dev had a practical nature and did not resent that Rai had not paid him the ₹2 lakhs. Goldie was not bothered about the payment that he did not receive, but was hurt that Rai had gone back on his word. He never told anyone about his feelings. (It was only while talking for this book that he opened up).

The movie did very well but a few lawyers from Lucknow, Kanpur and some other towns filed a case against it for being bold, claiming it was harming the society. Rai was worried when he received the notice. It was then that Goldie came to know of the tricks used by lawyers from small towns. It was their way of making some money. Some money exchanged hands and the matter was dropped.

Rai's fortunes changed with *Johny Mera Naam*. The production cost was ₹60 lakhs while the movie, in nine months, made more than ₹3 crore. As Goldie had refused to work with him, he took the help of Yash Chopra to launch *Joshila*. Those days Yash used to work with his elder brother, B.R. Chopra. Rai could not separate Goldie from Dev but it can be said that he succeeded in doing that with the Chopras.

❖❖❖

Hurt by Gulshan Rai's behavior, Goldie decided to produce a movie of his own. It would be a hundred percent his, he decided. He had heard a story on corruption in the medical field from author Kaushal Bharati. Goldie had bitter experiences during his kidney operation and had heard sad tales from his relatives too. So interested was he in the subject of corruption among doctors that he worked on the screenplay himself.

At the silver-jubilee party thrown for the success of *Guide*, Dev Anand was the star attraction while Goldie was ignored. Everyone wanted to be around Dev and as Goldie roamed alone, a woman approached him and asked,

'You made *Guide*, didn't you?'

Goldie recognized the young woman as actress Mumtaz. While watching the rushes of *Teesri Manzil*, she had brought food for Goldie and they had chatted a little. Goldie had realized that she was star material and not fit to do roles with Dara Singh. But Goldie had not been able to find an appropriate role for her in *Jewel Thief* or *Johny Mera Naam*. Goldie decided to cast Mumtaz in his own film.

'Papa, what is your view on casting Mumtaz?' Goldie asked Dev.

'I don't think she will fit the role.' Dev was not willing to take Dara Singh's co-star as the heroine of his film. Goldie was insistent and asked Dev to consider the matter later, leaving it for the time being.

At Navketan Films, Goldie had always done side roles. He was a good actor and wanted to play the lead. Keeping that in mind, he created the character of Jagannath Kothari, ensuring that the role did not overshadow that of Dev's.

Goldie, while reading out the story, had told Dev about his role. Dev could not object to it openly and so gave his consent. The character Goldie had created was such that it shone on screen despite the fact that Goldie would ensure giving Dev maximum camera time. The film was *Tere Mere Sapne*. Dev did not like the fact that Goldie's role was becoming prominent. This worried Goldie as he didn't want Dev Papa to feel that he was trying to usurp his position or compete with him.

Goldie had taken Hema Malini as a guest star in the movie. It was Hema Malini's large-heartedness that she agreed to a guest role and did not bother to ask about her role or discuss money matters. Mumtaz, though, was upset seeing a star in the film. She wondered if her role would get diminished.

'Don't bother about others, Mumtaz,' Goldie explained. 'I needed a star character, hence I have taken Hema.'

Mumtaz did a fine job though the movie did not do well at the box office. Viewers did not accept Mumtaz in a serious role.

There were also allegations that the movie was copied from an English novel, *The Citadel*. But Goldie refuted the same, stating that the latter half was totally different. Goldie's role was praised by critics, much to his embarrassment as he did not want Dev to be upset. Goldie was sensitive to other people's sentiments but he wondered if people bothered about what he thought! The movie may not have done well commercially but it has the 'Goldie' touch. He has shown the most intimate scenes with sensitivity, thus making them look natural and yet not cheap.

❖❖❖

Goldie's nephew Gogi Anand worked as an assistant director and another nephew, Yash Kohli, worked as production controller. Yash was keen to produce, while Gogi, having studied at the Film and Television Institute in Pune, wanted to become a director. They both decided to launch a movie, but could not afford Dev Anand, a star and an expensive one at that. They then approached Manoj Kumar, but his calendar was busy. It would have been the same case with any big star. This is when they turned to Goldie.

Goldie had always loved to act and his small roles had been received well. None of the famous actresses were willing to pair opposite Goldie, as they preferred established actors or a large banner to work under. It was something Goldie was unaware of. Later, actresses like Nutan and Asha Parekh worked with Goldie in *Main Tulsi Tere Aangan Ki*, a film under Raj Khosla's banner. Rekha, a newcomer, did not have any qualms working with Goldie. She fit the role well and Goldie signed her for the film; they became good friends later.

The story was nothing extraordinary. It was about a person with a split personality. The movie was titled *Double Cross*. Goldie wrote the screenplay based on a story written by Suraj Sanim. They wrote the dialogues together.

Despite it being Gogi's first movie – this was around

1972 – Goldie never interfered for the eight months of the shoot. Goldie had a good sense of timing but his face was not expressive and romantic. He could not see well without his glasses. Gogi made the mistake of making Goldie wear a wig which did not suit him at all.

The trials were well received by the distributors, making Goldie confident of a positive audience response. Mangesh Desai, the sound recordist, pronounced the movie a hit, saying it would launch Vijay Anand as a star. But Gogi was skeptical about its success. Even today he is not able to say why he felt so. It might have been his intuition. For various reasons, including the fact that Goldie was not exactly a star, the movie did not do well, except in the first week of its launch.

Gogi did not put the blame on Goldie and admits that the story was not great to begin with. He says the movie was not a total flop and that everyone earned a little money. The movie did run a little in Bombay and Calcutta. It did not run at all in places like Uttar Pradesh and Delhi.

❖❖❖

Tere Mere Sapne did not do well in Punjab, which upset the distributors. In order to pacify them, Goldie decided to make a movie with Dev; that is how *Chhupa Rustam* was announced. 'Dev Anand as *Chhupa Rustam*' created a buzz among the distributors. After a lot of deliberation, Goldie decided on a screenplay. The story was simple – it was about a hunt for gold treasure. *Mackenna's Gold* had released in India and Goldie, so that people did not accuse him of blatantly copying that film, added a lot of other characters and side stories. The story was about an international mafia eyeing treasure in the Mohenjo-daro and Harappa ruins. It featured an archaeologist in search of the ruins. Goldie was clear that the movie had to be commercially successful. He was not looking for artistic satisfaction here. The movie fared well in the box office, helping him to clear the debts of *Tere Mere Sapne*. It also helped Dev Anand's career graph to rise once again.

Goldie made the mistake of acting in *Chhupa Rustam*, not something Dev Anand appreciated. Dev had actually walked off in a huff during the shoot of a *qawwali* song when he came to know that the Goldie was part of it.

His objection was, 'I am the hero! Why is the song being picturized on Goldie?'

An upset Goldie decided, for the sake of completing the film, to shoot the song with only Dev, and duly informed Dev that he had reduced his own role. Only then Dev returned to the set. (Dev had put Chetan Anand in a fix similarly, when he refused to give further dates for *Kinare Kinare* after it was nearly 90 per cent shot.)

Goldie reduced his role in the movie and created a new character, for which he chose Premnath.

Initially, there was only one villain enacted by Ajit. Now with the introduction of Premnath, the story had become complicated. Added to it was Dev's attitude. It all led to a diminishing interest for Goldie in the movie, but he finally managed to complete the shooting. His interest in the entire aspect of filmmaking too was declining. He continued to fulfil his desire for acting by doing movies that did not feature Dev, even acting in Chetan's *Hindustan Ki Kasam*.

❖❖❖

Goldie was an admirer of Chetan Anand's writing and direction. *Hindustan Ki Kasam* had the Indo-Pakistan war as a backdrop. Goldie was not comfortable with Chetan's preference for actress Priya Rajvansh, who had starred in another war film, *Haqeeqat*. From the first, Goldie felt *Hindustan Ki Kasam* would suffer if Priya played a double role in it. He later believed that the movie would have done better had she not been in the movie! He found the idea of the heroine being shown as a spy quite laughable. The audience rejected her and the movie did not do well. Goldie believed that someone like Nargis would have been a better fit, and could have possibly made the film successful.

Goldie had realized during the making of *Haqeeqat* that the relationship between Chetan and Priya was getting intimate. Chetan started taking her in all his movies, irrespective of whether she fit the role or not. In Goldie's words, 'Priya Rajvansh was a disaster for Chetan Anand's films.'

Goldie had tried convincing Chetan that Priya was just an ordinary actor, but his suggestions were ignored, and Chetan was miffed enough to stop discussing scripts with Goldie. He even requested Goldie to make a movie starring Priya, hoping his magic touch would launch her into stardom, but Goldie was reluctant to take her. Of course, he couldn't bluntly tell his elder brother about his feelings. He tried to escape from the situation by suggesting a script where Priya was a mute character. As expected, Chetan did not pursue Goldie further on the subject. Chetan was aware of Priya's shortcomings, but his love for her made him overlook everything. Despite knowing that the audience kept rejecting her, he continued taking her in his movies. He did not want to offend her in any manner.

❖❖❖

Goldie had often bumped into producer-director Manoj Kumar and director Prakash Mehra in Kalyanji-Anandji's music room while working on the songs for *Johny Mera Naam*. Those days Prakash was struggling to make his mark. Goldie often met star-actor Dilip Kumar, too, during discussions on the songs of his movie, *Gopi*. Dilip Kumar knew Goldie since his childhood days and secretly admired his work as a director. Goldie had heard that Dilip Kumar had specially ordered a print of *Guide* to see while shooting in Madras.

One day, while they sat chatting in the music room, Dilip Kumar praised Goldie,

'Kalyanji, you don't know this boy's capabilities!'

'I am aware! He may look young but he packs a punch.'

Dilip Kumar pulled Goldie's hand and, in a friendly gesture, threw him on the ground and sat on his chest. He said,

'Will you make a movie with me? Tell me!'

'Yusuf bhai, I will do as you say. Just command me! I will present myself when you say so,' Goldie said, smiling.

'I want to know the technique behind your songs. What goes on in your mind?'

'I will tell you, but please let me get up now,' Goldie pleaded.

Dilip Kumar laughed and let him go. Goldie was enamoured by Dilip Kumar's childlike enthusiasm. He had never shown any starry behaviour.

Dilip Kumar and the Anands had been family friends for years. Dilip Kumar's elder brother Ayub Khan was Chetan's friend and the other brother, Nasir Khan, was close to Dev. They had started their journey in the film industry together. Dilip Kumar's elder sister Saeeda was Goldie's sister's friend. The families met regularly. Goldie was friends with Dilip Kumar's younger brothers, Aslam and Alam. Dilip Kumar would never visit Dev's home though. This was when Dev had just got a job at Prabhat Films, and Dilip Kumar was at Bombay Talkies. Dev was starting his career while Dilip Kumar had already done a few films.

Goldie was in school when he saw the movie, *Tarzan*. His curiosity was tickled seeing some underwater shots. He asked Dilip Kumar, when he went to his house a few days later, 'How does one take an underwater shot?' He presumed Yusuf bhai would know; after all, he worked in the movies!

'It is a secret,' Dilip Kumar answered.

The young Goldie believed Dilip Kumar and didn't bother to question him again. When he himself entered the film industry, he realized that it was not a secret but just a technique. He also realized that Dilip Kumar did not know about it and had called it a secret to hide his ignorance!

After the success of *Johny Mera Naam*, Goldie wanted to make a movie starring Dilip Kumar, Dev Anand and Raj Kapoor together.

Those days producer duo Mushir-Riaz (Mushir Alam and

Mohammad Riaz) had become popular with the launch of *Safar*. They also launched Dilip Kumar-starrer *Bairaag* but were keen to produce a big-budget movie. Goldie was then a much sought-after director and, as expected, Mushir-Riaz approached him for their project.

'It should be a big-budget film,' they told Goldie.

'This is the age of stars and I am sure if we make a movie with three stars, it would be a big one,' Goldie suggested. 'All we need is a script that will excite the three of them.'

'We are scared to approach Dilip sahab. Why don't you get the three of them to agree?' the producers suggested.

Goldie knew that Dev Anand was not happy with his experience while working with Dilip Kumar on the sets of *Insaniyat*. When he broached the topic, Dev said, 'There is no doubt Dilip sahab is a great actor but he interferes a lot. He changes the script after discussing with the scriptwriter. If you are confident of handling him and ensuring that he does not interfere, I am fine to sign up.'

'I am the writer and director and if I cannot ensure a balance between the three stars, there is no point in making the movie,' Goldie assured Dev.

Goldie approached Dilip Kumar next and was pleasantly surprised to get his acceptance for the proposed movie. The question was to get Raj Kapoor to accept. He was a well-known star and director, but Goldie was sure that he would not refuse to work with the other two stars. Goldie knew that Raj Kapoor directed sensitive movies but at the same time was commercially conscious when working under other directors. But Goldie had a different experience.

A character actor called Krishna Dhawan, working with Prithvi Theatre, had done many movies under the Navketan banner. He used to work with R.K Films and knew Raj Kapoor well. One day he called Goldie and said, 'Raj Kapoor sahab asked for a print of *Guide*, which he saw in the studio between 2 a.m. and 5 a.m. He really liked the movie.'

After a few months, Goldie and Raj Kapoor met at a party.

Goldie introduced himself, 'I am Dev's younger brother, Vijay Anand. I directed *Guide*.'

'Oh, is that so? How are you?' Raj Kapoor enquired politely and moved away.

Goldie was surprised that Raj Kapoor did not bother to say anything about *Guide*. A few days later he was told Raj Kapoor saw *Guide* once again in his studio at night and was all praise for the movie.

Goldie realized that Raj Kapoor was not keen to get acquainted. He asked Goldie every time they met, 'Oh, you are Dev's brother, aren't you?' Goldie had a similar experience with V. Shantaram. He too had ordered a print of *Guide* and seen it in his Rajkamal Studio but refused to recognize Goldie when they met. Goldie soon realized the two-faced behavior of many such people but he continued to give them respect for their age, experience and stature. He referred to Raj Kapoor as Raj sahab and V. Shantaram as Anna sahab.

Goldie did not want Raj Kapoor or Dilip Kumar to have a bias that Goldie as a scriptwriter would give Dev's role more importance. To avoid that, he decided not to be the scriptwriter. Those days the duo Salim-Javed was very popular. Their *Sholay* had been a super hit. Goldie said, when he briefed the duo, 'Write a story and screenplay that balance the roles of Dilip Kumar and Dev Anand. And the person holding the balance should be Raj Kapoor.'

After ten or twelve meetings, the story was developed. It was based on the hit musical *West Side Story,* which was inspired by Shakespeare's *Romeo and Juliet,* but now in an Indianised form. It was about two gangsters in Mumbai. The railway line in the city dissects the east and west sides. One of the gangsters is the modern-day suave Romeo, while the other is a local guy in dhoti and chappals. The modern guy was to be Dev Anand and the local man Dilip Kumar. The unwritten rule was to run their businesses in their respective areas and never cross over to the other side, lest they get killed. While they are cut-throat enemies, the modern guy falls in love with the sister of the local man, the Juliet to his Romeo. He does not know that she is the local guy's sister. The two realize the truth soon and when the local guy professes to kill his sister and her lover, the enmity between the two increases. The poor sister is pulled between the two rivalries, unable to decide her loyalties.

Then she gets kidnapped. Both are shocked and suspect each other. This is where Raj Kapoor is introduced, a character based on Birbal. He is shown as a practical man who knows them both. He tells them that they both loved the girl as a sister and a lover, respectively, but the man who has kidnapped her is stronger than them. He convinces them to bury their enmity and work together to find her. They both now work hand in hand saving each other's lives while searching for the girl. As expected, they rescue her and Dev Anand gets married to Dilip Kumar's sister.

Dev wanted Goldie to ensure that his role was not diminished and Goldie promised him the same. Dilip Kumar heard the script but did not react. Instead, he asked Goldie to listen to another story he had in mind. Naturally, the role there was heavily tilted in Dilip Kumar's favour. Goldie realized that his project for the stars to work together was unlikely to see the light of day. He met Mushir and asked him to drop the project.

One day Kalyanji, while chatting with Dilip Kumar, asked, 'Why does a great actor like you look into the aspects of direction on the sets?'

'Why would I bother to interfere if I have a great director to direct me? Unfortunately, that is not the case,' he justified.

A.R. Kardar, when asked by Goldie why he was not on the sets while his film was being shot, merely shrugged his shoulders and said, 'Dilip Kumar holds the reins of the movie. What is the point in me being present there?'

Goldie was surprised to hear an experienced and well-known director-producer like Kardar say that.

Goldie believed that each and every actor should leave it to the director to direct – whether the actor was Dilip Kumar, Dev Anand or Marilyn Monroe. He believed it was the director's right to do his job and the actor should repose complete faith in him. He knew that an actor's interference would destroy the balance of the script. Goldie had planned his script keeping the stars in mind. Dilip Kumar had by then released *Ganga Jamuna*. Goldie wanted Dilip Kumar to play the local *goonda* with Vyjayanthimala as his sister. Raj Kapoor had by then become quite obese and the role suited him. Dev Anand, dapper and handsome, was the perfect romantic lead.

But all that came to naught and the project never took off. It would have been a sure success with three great stars on screen. Goldie believed that any movie with Dev Anand and Dilip Kumar would have been a hit. But his dream remained unfulfilled.

❖❖❖

Goldie was contemplating a new script when producer Vinod Doshi approached him to direct a movie. Goldie had an interesting story with him – that of a simple girl and a sentimental lover with common friends who take advantage of them. Goldie had not directed a movie for a producer outside Navketan since *Teesri Manzil*. He did not refuse Doshi's offer; he had debts after *Tere Mere Sapne*. The movie proposed by Doshi was titled *Blackmail*. Those days Dharmendra used to be in touch with Goldie. He knew Goldie had the reputation of being a brilliant director. Goldie decided to take Dharmendra for the hero's role. In 1970, the Dharmendra-Raakhee starrer *Jeevan Mrityu* had done well. Raakhee was a good actor too. Goldie decided to take her as the female lead. Goldie felt that Shatrughan Sinha, who was then known for his negative roles, would suit a character with grey shades.

Goldie wanted Kishore Sahu to play the role of a scientist but he was busy elsewhere and Goldie selected Madan Puri for the same.

After the casting, Goldie focused on the music with Kalyanji-Anandji. Songs like *Asha o Asha, Main doob doob jaata hoon*, and *Mile, mile do badan*, were finalized one after another in quick succession. Rajendra Krishan was the lyricist.

Goldie wanted a love song. He described the situation to the music duo:

> The hero is unable to express his love to the heroine. He is shy and barely manages to speak when the two meet. He writes a letter each day but is scared to post them. One day he finds the courage to give her the letters, saying they express his feelings. The heroine reads the letters and the song is created.

Kalyanji was not convinced. How could the letters be a song?

'That is the beauty. I want a song here. The hero and heroine are not singing but it is the letters!'

Despite quite a few sittings, they were unable to get the lyrics. The song was to be picturized in Ooty. Before leaving for Ooty, Goldie sat with the music duo to get the tune finalized. The words should express the emotions of the hero.

It was nearly midnight when Goldie suggested,

'How about the words: *Pal pal dil ke paas tum rahti ho?*'

Anandji immediately set it to tune when Goldie added, '*Jeevan meethi pyaas yeh kahti ho.*' The song was on its way!

The next day Goldie apologized to Rajendra Krishna, saying he was not a writer. 'You see if the words seem fit and take it further,' he said modestly.

Rajendra Krishna wanted the initial lines to remain as they were and started working on the other stanzas.

Goldie had to go to Ooty before the song was recorded. The question was whether to shoot the song without a background score. He asked Dharmendra to hum the lyrics while he shot. No one would believe seeing the song that it was shot without the original song being available for the shooting.

Rakhi was pregnant and it was impossible to get dates that matched with Dharmendra's. Despite such challenges, Goldie managed to complete the shooting as per schedule. By the time the movie was released, many things had changed. From a romantic hero, Dharmendra was becoming popular as an action hero. This impacted the success of the movie. Madan

(L to R) At the premier of *Johny Mera Naam*: Producer Gulshan Rai, and guests B.R. Chopra, Dev Anand, Hema Malini, Goldie, Jeevan and others

Dev Anand and Hema Malini in *Johny Mera Naam*

Dev Anand and Hema Malini in *Johny Mera Naam*

Mumtaz and Goldie at the premier of *Tere Mere Sapne*

Goldie and Dev Anand in *Tere Mere Sapne*

Dharmendra and Raakhee in *Blackmail*

At the *muhurat* of *Jaan Hazir Hai*:
Prem Kishan, Premnath and Goldie

Director Raj Khosla, Asha Parekh and Goldie
on the sets of *Main Tulsi Tere Angan Ki*

Amitabh Bachchan and Goldie on the sets of *Ram Balram*

Ketan Anand and Goldie editing *Hum Rahe Na Hum*

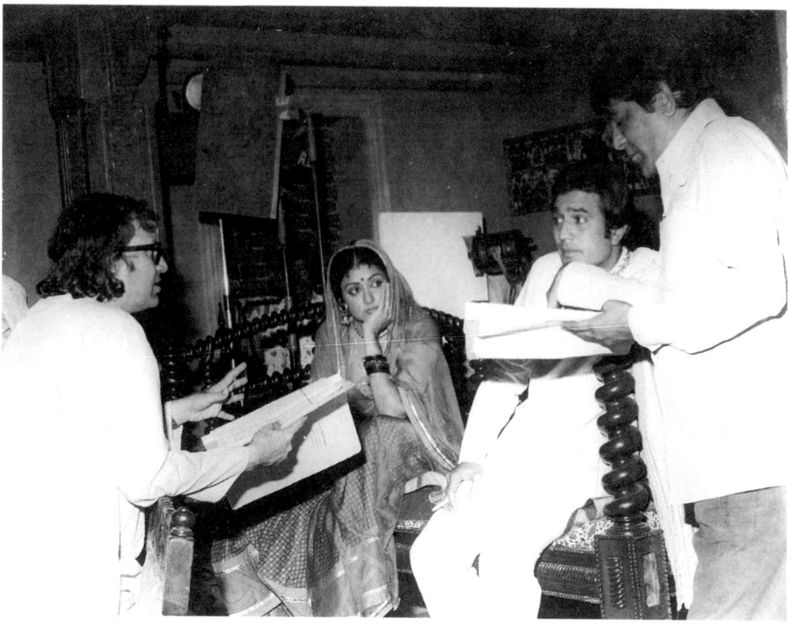

Directing Hema Malini and Rajesh Khanna for *Rajput*

Goldie and Leena Chandavarkar in *Chor Chor*

Having fun on the sets of the TV series *Tehkikaat*:
Karan Razdan, Ashok Kumar and Goldie

Goldie playing the harmonium gifted to him by
the legendary music director, Sachin Dev Burman

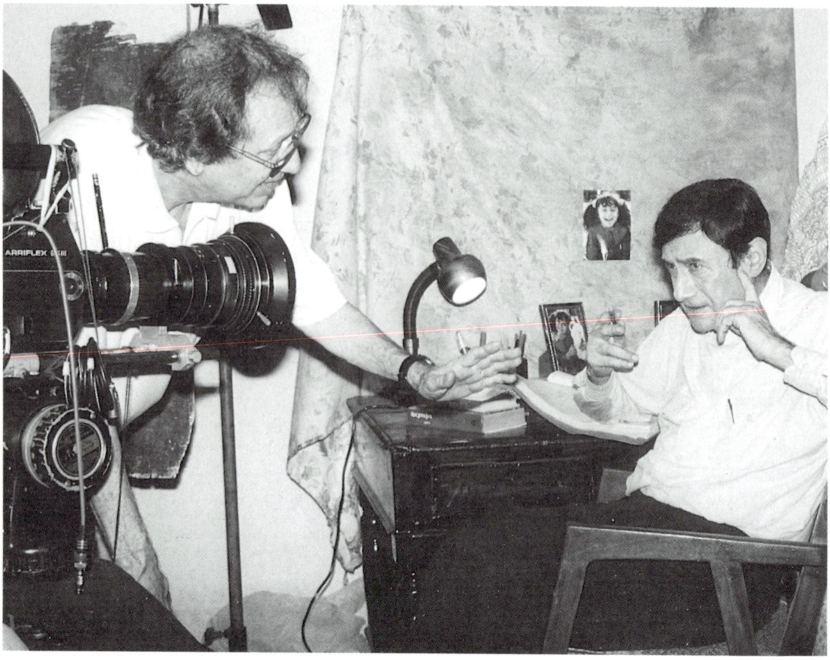

Goldie and Dev Anand during the shooting
of their last film together – *Jana Na Dil Se Dur*

The brothers Anand – Goldie, Dev and Chetan Anand

Puri, used to being seen in the role of a villain, was not accepted as a scientist. Despite being a well-made movie, it did not do well at the box office.

❖❖❖

Both *Agra Road* and *Double Cross* with Goldie as the lead actor failed at the box office. His performances in *Kala Bazar, Tere Mere Sapne* and *Haqeeqat* garnered a lot of praise, though he was not the hero in these films. Goldie wished that a film with him in the lead or with him as the central character would do well. Luckily, he got an opportunity soon enough. It was from director Anil Ganguly.

'This is Anil Ganguly speaking.'

'Anil Ganguly who?' Goldie asked.

'We don't know each other. I am new to this industry.'

'What is it about? I am not directing films at present,' Goldie said.

'It's not about direction. I want to speak to you about a hero's role.'

Goldie was a little taken aback.

'Who is the heroine?'

'Jaya Bhaduri.'

'Okay. Please come and meet me tomorrow,' Goldie said.

This was in 1972. A Bengali film based on the Bengali classic novel *Saat Paake Bandha,* by Ashutosh Mukhopadhyay had Suchitra Sen and Soumitra Chatterjee playing the lead roles. Produce Sanath Kothari planned to make a Hindi remake of the film. Anil Ganguly had just come into the Hindi film industry then. Goldie was not their first choice for the film. They had signed Vinod Khanna but hadn't decided on the film they wanted to make with him. Vinod was trying to get rid of his image as a villain and become a hero. Anil Ganguly was not sure of the audience accepting Vinod in a professor's role owing to his villainous image. Jaya Bhaduri suggested Romesh

Sharma's name for the hero's role, (Romesh Sharma acted with Jaya in *Doosri Sita* and had also produced the film *Hum* with Amitabh Bachchan later on) but Anil Ganguly felt that Romesh Sharma was too young for a professor's role.

Those days, no mainstream actor was ready to don spectacles in films. Moreover, the film had a woman-centric subject, and no hero was ready to sign up for it. Actor Navin Nischol had just stepped into the film industry then, but decided not to do the film because of its woman-centric subject. While Sanath Kothari and Anil Ganguly were wondering about whom to cast as the hero, someone remarked that they needed a hero who looked like Vijay Anand, who wore glasses in *Tere Mere Sapne*.

When Goldie heard the story, he realized it was a female-centric story and wasn't keen on doing it. But when Anil Ganguly said that if the film did not have the professor's character it will make no sense, Goldie agreed. He felt that Kothari's director had to be someone who could remake the film with the same essence as the Bengali original. The reason why Kothari had chosen Anil Ganguly was because he was a Bengali, but Anil wasn't fluent in Hindi and Kothari needed someone who could guide Ganguli if there was some mistake. That was another reason why he had chosen Goldie.

'Why don't you watch the Bengali film once?' Kothari suggested.

'No, I won't. I don't want to be influenced by that film,' Goldie refused outright.

Goldie felt that they need not copy the Bengali film frame to frame and asked them to create a new script with new situations and characters suitable for the Hindi film.

The screenplay writer, M.G Hashmat, worked on the script with Goldie. The Hindi version was called *Kora Kagaz*.

The *muhurat* for the film was held at Natraj Studio. Producer-director Shakti Samanta's film, *Anuraag*, was being shot there the same day, and Anil Ganguly invited Rajesh Khanna and Shakti Samanta for the muhurat shot. The shot featured Jaya Bhaduri and Goldie.

The shooting started immediately thereafter. The set for Jaya Bhaduri's house had been created for the first schedule. Apart from Goldie, Jaya Bhaduri, Achala Sachdev, A.K. Hangal, Nazneen and some others were present. Goldie had only four days of work in the first schedule.

Jaya respected Goldie a lot. She had just graduated from the film institute at Pune and had made her debut in *Guddi*. She would not listen to Anil Ganguly's instructions, instead asking Goldie for his opinion on a particular shot or a scene.

Goldie had written most of his scenes with some help from Hashmat. *Kora Kagaz* was Anil Ganguly's first film; he found it difficult to explain the scenes in Hindi. Character actress Achala Sachdev, who played Jaya's mother in the film, had to speak while climbing steps. Anil was not happy with the shot and took a few retakes. But he was not able to tell Achala clearly where she was going wrong, which irritated her. Finally, he called Goldie for help. Goldie suggested, 'Achalaji, you seem to be tense. Relax, and as you go up a few steps, say the lines. Stop again, take a few steps and say your dialogues.'

Achala did exactly what Goldie asked her to do and the shot was okayed immediately.

Goldie was against Anil Ganguly's idea of shooting a few flashback scenes. He was also against the idea of the song, *Mera jeevan kora kagaz,* being a background score, wanting it to be picturised as the hero singing it. Goldie had suggested a situation to Anil where the hero would be sitting under a tree singing the song when the heroine arrives. But the producer and the financiers did not agree.

Kora Kagaz was only half complete when some misunderstandings developed between producer Sanath Kothari and the distributor, halting the shooting midway. A few months elapsed and the shooting resumed but by then Jaya was pregnant, delaying the honeymoon song Goldie and Jaya were to shoot together. It was important now to complete the remaining portions as quickly as possible. Jaya did not appreciate the way the film had turned out and started losing interest. She was refusing dates for the climax scene. Finally, Sanath asked Goldie for help.

Eager to complete the shooting, Goldie requested Jaya to come for just one day.

She came for the shooting but was in a foul mood.

'This scene is very long and will need at least three shifts to shoot,' she complained.

Hashmat had, as usual, written long scenes.

Goldie pitched in. 'Don't go by what is written. I will tell you the lines. You just perform the way you feel is right.'

Goldie and Jaya completed the scene, and it turned out to be the highlight of the film.

The music was by Kalyanji-Anandji and the songs had been penned by Hashmat. For some reason he had been unable to come up with a title song and Kalyanji suggested that he should speak to Goldie about it. He met Goldie at Filmistan Studio where he was shooting for *Chhupa Rustam*.

Those days the song, *Kora kagaz tha yeh man mera,* from Shakti Samanta's film *Aradhana* was a rage. Goldie took a thread from that song and suggested to Hashmat that he should write a song that talked about life being a blank piece of paper and sometimes remains blank till the end. The song, *Mera jeevan kora kagaz,* soon took shape.

The same Hashmat directed a film called *Shaktishali* a few years later in which Goldie played the role of a professor. Ashok Kumar, who played the role of a principal, did not like Hashmat's long, flowery dialogues, and asked Goldie to do the job.

Although Goldie was associated with *Kora Kagaz* only as an actor, he did help Anil Ganguly with the editing as well. The film finally got completed and was declared a super hit on the first day of the release itself. It was a pleasant surprise for everyone, including Goldie. His acting was applauded by all.

Confident that the audiences would accept him as the hero, Goldie decided to produce *Chor Chor.* He handed the reins of directing to his first assistant director, Prem Prakash. Leena Chandavarkar was the heroine. Lakshmikant and Pyarelal were supposed to compose the music. The film was completed in six months and there were some situations kept for songs. But even as the discussions for the song recording were on with Lakshmikant-Pyarelal, the other musician artists went on a strike that carried on for three months. It was a murder mystery, so Goldie decided to release the movie without songs, though he had written the songs . The audience rejected Goldie as a hero and the movie bombed at the box office, leaving him heartbroken.

❖❖❖

Goldie was losing interest with filmmaking and the film industry day by day. He was hurt and disappointed by the negative experiences he had while making films. Even Dev Anand had refused to put *'Vijay Anand presents'* in *Hum Dono,* and the problems he had to face with Dev during the making of *Chhupa Rustam...* All these experiences deepened the disagreements between the brothers and made Goldie think that the world was selfish, indifferent and superficial. People behaved one way while getting films made by him but changed colours as soon as the film was over and forgot their promises and commitments. Goldie had been hurt by Dev, but being ten years younger, he couldn't say anything to his brother. Goldie felt that Dev expected him to do exactly as told. Sleep eluded Goldie for nights on end. He was a sensitive soul, after all! He was hurt by the fact that however hard he worked, others seemed to be getting the benefit or credit for it.

It was during the shooting of *Johny Mera Naam* that an ascetic known to Premnath came to the sets. Looking at Goldie for a few moments, he said, 'This man is like the engine of a railway train. He just drives the train... He has no idea how many people reach their destination riding on his train. And like the engine gets no credit for it, nobody will give him credit for his work.'

The prediction had come out true. While Goldie was in this state of mind, a person entered his life and, unintentionally, his disillusionment deepened further.

It was during the recording of the songs for *Johny Mera Naam*. One day Kalyanji called Goldie.

'Goldie, can you come to my music room if you are free? I want to introduce you to someone.'

Goldie did not know his life was going to change. When he reached the music room, he found a bearded man in a dhoti and bare upper body sitting there.

'This is Acharya Rajneesh. He has studied philosophy and spirituality deeply.' Kalyanji said.

Goldie's love for spirituality had grown over the years and he had read a lot of books. He prayed and performed pujas regularly. He would be immersed in his work while he was shooting a film but once he returned home he would drown in his books on spirituality. He contemplated deeply and meditate. He would go to the beach and sit there in peace and solitude.

Once the formal introductions were done, Rajneesh started speaking on spirituality. Goldie was blown away by Rajneesh's impressive personality, his spiritual knowledge and wisdom.

When Goldie got up to leave after about three hours, Rajneesh said, 'Do you have time in the evening? If you don't have anything important, I am giving a discourse at the Azad Maidan.'

Goldie went that day and was hooked. He attended the discourses for five consecutive days and on the sixth day invited Rajneesh to his house. Rajneesh accepted the invitation and came to Goldie's house and later left for Jabalpur, his home. Rajneesh was teaching philosophy in a college in Jabalpur those days. Rajneesh would stay at the Cricket Club of India's guest rooms whenever he visited Bombay.

Goldie met Rajneesh whenever he was in the city. Rajneesh continued visiting Bombay frequently for the next two to three years and he would leave his books on spirituality for his followers.

Three years later, Rajneesh moved to Bombay and started living in a flat in Woodland Apartments on Cumbala Hill. Goldie was greatly influenced by Rajneesh and now that Rajneesh lived in Mumbai, Goldie visited his house almost every day. No one was allowed into Rajneesh's private room. He met his visitors only in the living room. He would read for eighteen hours sitting in his room.

Once on a visit to Rajneesh's house, Goldie suggested going out for a ride but Rajneesh declined politely and said, 'Instead of going out, let's sit here and read,' and handed Goldie a book to read.

Goldie was under Rajneesh's spell. The two of them would discuss varied topics from Buddha to Krishna. Goldie's dream of understanding Buddha, Mahavir, Rama and Krishna came true. Goldie always felt that despite having everything, there was something amiss and he wanted to find that. He wanted to know why we are born and why we die.

When he returned to his own world after meeting Rajneesh, he would feel as if he had come to a very selfish place full of negative people. On the contrary, most of the people who came to Rajneesh seemed intelligent and creative. Some were musicians while others were litterateurs, architects... but hardly anyone from the film industry. There was a healthy interaction and exchange of ideas whenever Goldie met these people. It was only much later that Goldie said, 'Only the garbage visit Rajneesh now.'

Rajneesh had himself predicted this and said in one of his talks. Goldie felt that Rajneesh had a vast knowledge of philosophy and spirituality and was as great as Swami Vivekananda. One day, Rajneesh invited Goldie to an eleven-day retreat he was conducting at Mount Abu.

A lot of people, including the family that had given Rajneesh their Bombay flat, were supposed to go to Mount Abu. Rajneesh would deliver a short talk at six in the morning and then teach them how to meditate. He would make his disciples meditate five times a day. He would ask everyone to maintain silence and to avoid talking. Goldie was meditating all day and he maintained silence for all the eleven days.

When Goldie returned to Bombay after eleven days, he had changed inside out. He had no idea how, but what he couldn't understand by reading books was now clear to him. Goldie had read the Upanishads, Gita, and many other texts, but had understood only their literal meaning; after discussing with Rajneesh, he could understand the deeper meaning of these texts. The light of knowledge had been lit in Goldie's mind and that reflected in every aspect of his life – be it filmmaking, writing and interaction with people. He seemed to be going through an existential crisis and he introspected deeply about every action of his. Another reason for his disillusionment was that he had fallen in love with his niece Sushma, his older sister's daughter. Though heard of in South India, this was against societal norms in North India where an uncle is not allowed to marry his niece. Sushma and Goldie, eight years apart, were very close to each other. Sushma had observed that though Goldie was the youngest, everyone in the Anand family consulted him on various issues. She, too, would discuss her college issues and other problems with Goldie. Both of them felt a deep friendship with each other.

When Goldie began looking for a bride on the insistence of his sister, he would come home and talk to Sushma about the girl he met, but subconsciously he was comparing the girl with Sushma. Sushma too felt a twinge of pain in her heart every time he spoke of or praised another girl. Soon, Goldie and Sushma realized that they were in love, and the news of their relationship spread in the Anand household. They faced a lot of opposition as no one could accept an uncle marrying his niece. Dev Anand refused to believe the story and berated family members for casting such aspersions. Dev told this author that he was very angry when he came to know about Sushma and Goldie's relationship.

Goldie was very confused and didn't know whether his love for Sushma was right or not. He was hesitant to go against his family, but also wanted to marry her. Sushma was not ready to marry Goldie, after facing rampant disapproval from her family. She too must have felt it was not right for her to fall in love with her uncle; but Goldie could not think about any other girl. He became further withdrawn and sad.

Goldie consulted Rajneesh. 'I meditate so much, read spiritual texts and yet I am not at peace,' Goldie confessed.

'Till you make a commitment to yourself, you will remain in this state. Whatever you do in life, you must be fully committed to it. You must be focused on what you desire. When a policeman stands at the traffic signal in his uniform, he is able to control the traffic. Without the uniform he is ignored and people break rules,' Rajneesh said.

'You wear these beads and see what happens,' Rajneesh said, putting on a string of rudrakasha beads around his neck. Goldie was stunned; he hadn't come there to wear beads or become an ascetic.

'This is the right thing to do,' said Rajneesh.

Goldie's disturbed state of mind didn't last long. There was a sudden change within him. He decided that now that he had worn the beads, he must accept them wholeheartedly. In any case he was tired of this world... so what was wrong if he became a sanyasi? 'Removing the beads would be like discarding my way of life,' Goldie told himself.

He became a disciple of Rajneesh from that day. He knew that people in the film industry would make fun of him and criticize him for his decision, but he was convinced that he had a right to live his life the way he wanted.

Within a month, Rajneesh asked Goldie to wear saffron clothes. Goldie started wearing saffron-coloured kurtas and lungis. People stopped inviting Goldie for parties. They cracked obscene jokes when he was around, but Goldie would simply walk away. Everyone may have been wondering what Goldie had done to himself, but Goldie gradually started enjoying the transformation he had undergone. Life had led him to the path of renunciation. He had always wanted to escape the hustle and bustle of daily life and the selfish behaviour of the people around him. He decided to stop acting and making films.

Goldie became so immersed in Rajneesh's way of life that he visited him every day, attended his camps and retreats and meditated a lot.

In the meantime, Rajneesh opened an ashram in Koregaon Park in Pune and Goldie went to live there on Rajneesh's advice. Chetan Anand, Dev Anand and his family members were very annoyed at Goldie's decision. They felt that Goldie was wasting all his talent and ruining his career by going with Rajneesh. Goldie was building a new studio at that time. He handed over the responsibility to his manager and left for the ashram in Pune.

He read a lot of books on spirituality and the scriptures there and mediated for almost eighteen hours a day. He had only two sets of clothes and wore wooden footwear. He felt very free and light because of the austere lifestyle. He was christened Vijay Bharati in the ashram.

He had a set routine. He would wake up early in the morning and meditate and follow it up with meditation every two hours. He would listen to Rajneesh's talks for an hour or so. Goldie was capable of immersing himself into any subject anyway and that came in handy at the ashram.

Goldie's nephew Ketan Anand, secretary Sooraj Salim, friend Mahesh Bhatt, and a few others followed Goldie to Pune and became Rajneesh's disciples. Actor Vinod Khanna, too, joined the ashram along with Mahesh Bhatt.

❖❖❖

Goldie had renounced everything; money or fame did not mean anything to him anymore. He did want to, however, put his money to good use. Worried about the future of his assistants, he wanted to make a movie so that they could earn some money.

Premnath's son Prem Krishen had assisted him in the making of *Chhupa Rustam* and *Blackmail*. Seeing his acting skills, Goldie decided to cast him in his movie. He selected a story written by his assistant Jyoti Swaroop, who was keen to direct the movie, but Manhar Nath Rangroo, the senior assistant director, was given the task. Shekhar Kapur was Goldie's sister's son, and Goldie decided to offer him an opportunity to act in the film. He recognized the talent of Kalyanji-Anandji's assistant Bal Parte, who organized the orchestra, and. gave him a chance to compose music. Goldie also gave a break to singer Dilraj Kaur.

Goldie started to search for a heroine. As everyone in the film was new, he wanted to take someone who was not a known face. Little did Goldie know that the film would be a turning point in his life, albeit for a short while.

Prem Krishen met Loveleen, a newcomer, at a party thrown for Vakil Babu. Loveleen was beautiful and, after having worked with a radio station in Delhi, had come to Bombay to try her luck in the film industry. Prem Krishen introduced her to Goldie, and soon they all passed the screen test. *Jaan Hazir Hai* was soon announced.

Goldie asked his assistant Prem Prakash to get a dress for Loveleen for the launch party. He then changed his mind and went out himself to buy the dress; after all his bitter experiences of the world, Goldie had fallen for the beautiful Loveleen. He probably believed that if he committed to someone and married her, he may be able to forget his love for Sushma.

The Rajneesh Ashram at Pune did not expect people to remain celibate. In fact, Rajneesh talked of celebrating life and living life to the fullest, and wanted his disciples to experience everything. Keeping all this in mind, Goldie decided to get married to Loveleen.

When he broached the topic with Sushma, she did not react. She had earlier refused Goldie's proposal and felt that she had no right to object to his decision.

With Loveleen's impending marriage to Goldie, he renewed his search for the heroine for his movie. Someone recommended Natasha, the niece of character actor Veena, and Goldie signed her on. The shooting began on 3 November, 1974. As Goldie was stationed at Pune, they chose several locations in the city for the shoot. Goldie was not the official director but continued to advise.

With the blessings of Acharya Rajneesh, on an auspicious day, Goldie and Loveleen got married. The reception was organized at Bombay's Oberoi Sheraton. After marriage, Goldie and Loveleen shifted to a bungalow near the ashram and came to Bombay whenever they felt like. Both had started wearing saffron clothes now.

Goldie did not devote himself fully to *Jaan Hazir Hai*, and his lack of total involvement showed in the end result. He was merely mentioned in the credits as 'Goldie presents', which did not have much of an impact. Goldie's dream of helping his assistants with a movie did not succeed the way he had imagined it to – he was not only running losses but also in debt. Malkan, the manager of Ketnav, had started behaving as if he owned the production house. Goldie suffered on two counts: financial disaster and an increasing domestic dissatisfaction.

Within a few months of marriage, Goldie realized that he and Loveleen were worlds apart. He had started comparing her with Sushma. Soon, minor disagreements started erupting daily that manifested into major arguments. Loveleen was ambitious and wanted to be a big star. Ketan Anand believed that was the reason she married Goldie. Loveleen soon realized that she had made a mistake by marrying Goldie.

Because of irreconcilable differences, the decided to separate. Goldie's spiritual journey was still on and he continued to divide his time between Pune and Bombay.

In the meanwhile, all kinds of riff-raff started visiting Rajneesh Ashram, and it became a place for hippies to hang out. It had become a den for free sex and drugs. Rajneesh's idea was to allow sex liberally so that a person gets over his or her physical desires – but the effect seemed to be quite opposite as people indulged freely. Vinod Khanna, too, had come here to get over his libido. Goldie noticed that sex was turning into an addiction at this place. Rajneesh's theory had come to naught, destroying many lives in the process.

Rajneesh introduced Goldie to a film star from England, suggesting that they stay together, much to Goldie's shock. Goldie took her around Pune, showing her the sights. When they returned to the ashram, Goldie told her, 'Lakshmi, I am not interested in free sex or anything else.'

In the meanwhile, Rajneesh's popularity was soaring and people were being charged ₹10 or 20 for a *darshan*. Memorabilia with Rajneesh's face were being sold, 'Rajneesh Nagar' was announced near Khandala, money was being collected in all ways possible. Quite like the way a film producer markets his movies, Rajneesh's team was marketing the mystery surrounding him and literally minting money.

❖❖❖

Goldie was almost suffocating in that atmosphere when Raj Khosla, who had earlier worked as a director with Navketan, came to meet him one day. He wanted Goldie to act in his movie, *Main Tulsi Tere Aangan Ki*. Raj Khosla had come to Bombay to be a playback singer but decided to try his hand at direction.

Goldie remembered meeting him when he was studying in St Xavier's College; despite their age difference, they had become good friends. Goldie had told him, 'Don't get flustered. We will give you a chance to work under Guru Dutt.'

Respecting Goldie's promise, Dev Anand had offered Raj Khosla a chance to work with Guru Dutt for *Baazi*.

Raj Khosla believed Goldie would suit the role in his movie well. While Goldie was not keen to return to the film world, he could not reject Raj Khosla's offer, worried that it may disappoint him.

Goldie was not happy in the ashram either, the way things were happening there. He started having self-doubts about his decision to leave the film industry and join the ashram. The lure of acting made him sign for the movie. After a gap of two years, Goldie had once again returned to the world of movies.

On the first day, Goldie met Asha Parekh and Nutan, his co-stars. Nutan stood up to receive him, hugging him affectionately. Raj Khosla was surprised. 'Don't make me jealous. I was about to introduce you two,' he said, laughing. The tuning between Nutan, Asha Parekh and Goldie led to a pleasant atmosphere on the sets. Goldie was not sure about the screenplay and expressed his doubts to Raj Khosla.

'Why don't you write the scenes? I am fine with that,' Raj Khosla suggested.

Goldie ended up doing most of the scriptwriting.

Raj Khosla would not come to the sets during shoots, leaving the direction to Goldie. He would come just to peep in at lunchtime, have a small chat and leave for the day. Goldie, thus, managed to direct most of the movie. He helped in the editing too.

While Vinod Khanna was the hero of the film, the role done by Goldie had more footage. It left Vinod Khanna miffed. Raj Khosla was in a spot. Vinod Khanna was a star and, without telling Goldie, he edited out many scenes featuring Goldie. And that too, in Goldie's own Ketnav Theatre. When Goldie came to know of this, he did not attend the premiere of the film and in fact, never watched the movie in his lifetime.

❖❖❖

Feeling fooled once again in life, Goldie returned to the ashram. But things were going from bad to worse here. He realized that every person wears a mask and that his life was a lie. Rajneesh's disciples were full of ego, trying to prove their supremacy over others. Inter-departmental quibbles had reached a frenzy. Spirituality was getting commercialized.

Goldie felt he had learnt what he intended to and that he did not have any further questions for Rajneesh. Even Rajneesh, he felt, seemed to be repeating himself and had nothing new to offer; he was now peddling views from other authors and spiritual gurus. His discourses were copied from many texts, which he put across as his original views. But he was a great speaker, with an ability to mesmerize his listener. Goldie was not comfortable in a world so artificial and false. He felt

Rajneesh did not deserve the praise the world was bestowing on him as a wise and intelligent man.

Maybe Rajneesh, too, sensed Goldie's discomfort. He advised Goldie to return to Bombay and start a meditation centre where he could give discourses.

Goldie may have had his private views about Rajneesh but his love for him had not disappeared. He converted the first floor of his editing and dubbing studio into a meditation centre.

He would conduct a three-hour meditation class in the evening after he spent the day reading and travelling, and visited Pune once a fortnight or so.

There was no dearth of Rajneesh's followers in Bombay and they found it convenient to come to Goldie's meditation centre. They would listen to Rajneesh's audio cassettes and ask Goldie their doubts. Goldie soon started recording his own cassettes. He had no desires left now. He did not aspire to achieve anything.

❖❖❖

In Navketan's silver-jubilee year, Dev Anand and Chetan Anand decided to set aside their differences with Goldie and launch a movie. Three movies were produced that year. *Jaaneman* was directed by Chetan and *Bullet* by was directed by Goldie, while Dev directed *Des Pardes*. Bullet starred Dev, Kabir Bedi and Parveen Babi, with Suraj Sanim as the scriptwriter. Kabir Bedi got good reviews as a villain, and debutante Jyoti Bakshi launched her career with the film. But with *Bullet* Goldie's downfall began. He seemed to have lost his magical touch. He had returned to the film world after three-and-a-half years. People wondered if he would return to the ashram at Pune or continue with his meditation centre in the city. Yet, his reputation preceded him and people queued up with projects. In order to brush them off, Goldie would demand a sum of ₹25 lakhs. Till then he had commanded a fee of ₹3 lakhs or ₹4 lakhs! Naturally, no producer was willing to shell out a such a amounts and Goldie did not get any projects.

But Goldie was pleasantly surprised when the producer duo Mushir-Riaz agreed to pay him the ₹25 lakhs he demanded. The producers wanted to make a grand multi-starrer using the recently introduced cinemascope technique.

Around this time, the then prime minister, the late Indira Gandhi had taken away the princely state of a prince in Saurashtra, because he patronised an infamous dacoit in the region, Diler Singh. Police had never been able to catch Diler Singh because of the royal patronage he enjoyed. Goldie decided to make a movie on this storyline. Goldie added a commercial angle that the hero, Rajesh Khanna, accepts his wife's son from an earlier affair. Goldie had encountered the ravines of Chambal while shooting for *Nau Do Gyarah.* He had heard back then of two men fighting for the custody of a boy. One was the biological father, the other the one who had raised him. He added this element to the story of *Rajput.* It was a sentimental story and Goldie wanted it to be one of his biggest hits.

Goldie wanted to show the undying spirit of the Rajputs. The story was about what love could achieve. Goldie, unfortunately, did not get the kind of time he wanted to make the movie – a single schedule was of twenty days at a stretch. Often, one of the two stars, Dharmendra or Rajesh Khanna, would be absent. Hema Malini's pregnancy caused a lot of delays. Vinod Khanna was at the Rajneesh Ashram and Goldie had to call him for his scheduled dates. Vinod Khanna was a reluctant actor then, more focused on his stay at Pune, while Rajesh Khanna was enamoured by his role.

Vinod Khanna's scenes were shot in Khandala, He would arrive there by two in the afternoon and leave within a few hours. After a few months, Vinod Khanna left for the US, leaving the film mid-way. He never bothered to inform Goldie or any other producer. Goldie and the producers were even willing to fly down to the US to finish shooting the pending scenes, but getting foreign exchange was a huge challenge. Finally, Goldie decided to reduce Vinod Khanna's scenes from the film, making changes to the script.

Goldie had written a special role with Premnath in mind but as he was busy with other commitments, Goldie had to take Ranjeet for the role. Just like Madan Puri did not fit into the role of a scientist in *Blackmail,* Ranjeet as a member of the royalty did not go down well with the audience.

Earlier, the producer duo had promised Goldie that they would shoot in Rajasthan but later they changed their mind and asked him to shoot at Film City in Goregaon. Half the sequence of the song, *Mere sang sang aaya teri yaadon ka mela,* was shot in the Film City studio. Goldie was being forced to compromise everywhere. He wanted a hundred coconut trees but had to make do with fifteen. Goldie realized that the movie was not being produced the way he had envisaged.

Goldie had learnt to adapt by now. A particular scene had to be shot against a blue sky, but he changed the script to suit accordingly when a blue sky or a clear day was not available.

Rajput, shooting for which began in 1977, was finally released in 1982. It did not do well even in Rajasthan against expectations. The fact that a woman gets pregnant out of wedlock and Vinod Khanna's love affairs with more than one person did not make the audience happy. Nevertheless, the film received a good response in Bihar, UP, Bengal and Bombay.

❖❖❖

Producer Tito wanted to make a comedy movie with depth. He, too, agreed to pay Goldie ₹25 lakhs, with a signing amount of ₹2.5 lakhs, to make *Ram Balram.* Actors Amitabh Bachchan and Dharmendra were signed on. Those days Amitabh used to charge ₹4 lakhs, and Dharmendra ₹6 lakhs. Zeenat Aman was signed for ₹3 lakhs. Rekha, who was close to Goldie those days, approached him, asking for a role in the movie.

'There is not much scope for a heroine as there are two heroes,' Goldie said.

'I want to work in a movie that you direct, that's all,' Rekha insisted.

Goldie agreed and Rekha was signed up for ₹2 lakhs.

Kamleshwar wrote the script for this light comedy: one hero is a policeman and the other a thief, who help each other. The story includes a lot of light-hearted moments.

Then, when the shooting for *Rajput* had just begun, a state of Emergency was declared in the country. The Censor Board took on a very strict outlook on what could be shown in a film and what couldn't, during this period. When Rajput was submitted with them for certification, it was impossible to convince the board that the policeman was helping his brother and sharing the spoils. Kamleshwar recommended changing the script to pass the censor board's requirement.

Goldie agreed and added another character in the form of a villain, an uncle of the two brothers, who makes them do wrong things. Amitabh takes his superiors into confidence and spreads a net to trap the uncle. But the main theme of the story was lost due to this change. It was one thing to show two brothers pairing up, and another to introduce a third person as the baddie. It was turning out to be a typical story about a good brother and a bad brother.

Another incident delayed the shooting by nearly eight months: Amitabh suffered from jaundice. The dates given by other actors were all wasted. By the time Amitabh recovered, Dharmendra got busy, finding it difficult to give dates. Those days Dharmendra was in great demand and would give only an hour or two for shoots. The next schedule began after eight months. In the meanwhile, with a few hits, Amitabh had achieved a super-star status and was receiving offers from many producers and directors. He was known for his discipline and was never late for any shoots. Dharmendra had started feeling a little jealous, seeing Amitabh's popularity. Amitabh was busy with *Mr. Natwarlal* when someone misled Dharmendra into believing that he was shooting for *Ram Balram*. Dharmendra was annoyed at that; how can they go ahead without me, he thought.

Goldie had worked with Dharmendra earlier but was surprised that Dharmendra had not asked him to clarify. He tried explaining the situation to Dharmendra but to no avail. Dharmendra's jealousy and his declining interest in the movie made it difficult for Goldie to synchronize the dates.

While they never expressed it openly, there was an ego problem between the two actors. They were too busy elsewhere and, in the short time they were on Goldie's set, they could not get under their character's skin. It was turning out to be a headache for Goldie.

It was critical to have both Dharmendra and Amitabh together for the song *Ik rasta do rahi*. The song needed the brothers to show their deep love for each other. Goldie found an innovative way out by shooting the scenes for both the actors separately. He decided to combine the scenes while editing the movie. No one knew when they saw the final outcome that the two had been shot separately.

Many industry people had written off Goldie but Goldie felt that his stay at the ashram had made him a more mature being; now he knew where to compromise and yet give the same result.

Goldie as a director knew the strengths and weaknesses of Amitabh and Dharmendra. He was aware that Amitabh was a much more gifted actor while Dharmendra had a handsome, charming persona. Dharmendra was loud while Amitabh was sensitive in his performances. Amitabh would listen to the scene carefully and give his best. He would do his homework and listen to the director's instructions. The two brothers meet their mother after a long time. Dharmendra, the thief, comes to know that the villain had tried to molest their mother. He vows to take revenge on him but Amitabh, the inspector, tries to stop him.

Amitabh reached the studio and asked Goldie regarding the shot. Goldie would normally send the dialogues a few days in advance but this time Amitabh was travelling and was not available. He asked Goldie to read the dialogues. Amitabh sensed that Goldie was in tears reading the lines. Goldie did not want Amitabh to get emotional while rehearsing the scene, and asked him to speak slowly. He didn't want Amitabh to do a perfect rehearsal. He wanted the emotions to come out during the final take.

When the Emergency was lifted, Goldie could contemplate getting the original screenplay back. But realizing that it would a humongous task to get dates and reshoot many scenes, he dropped the idea. The movie was finally ready.

Dharmendra troubled Goldie during the dubbing as well. At the back of his mind, Dharmendra was in awe and fearful of Amitabh and had started imitating him in voice. He would focus on his voice more than acting, which looked unnatural. While shooting he would speak in his own voice but would try to imitate Amitabh's husky voice in the dubbing studio. He would avoid dubbing if Goldie was around. Finally, Goldie stopped coming to the dubbing studio.

Ram Balram, initially slated to be completed in eight months, took seven years. They had shot for just 100 days in those seven years! Something similar had happened during the shooting of *Rajput,* too, leaving Goldie restless. Goldie believed a movie had to be contemporary, else the story can look jaded. The flops or hits of the actors' other movies also affected a movie being shot. Goldie consoled himself that the movie ran well. After all, he had invested a long time into it and was finally relieved.

❖❖❖

Goldie had accepted *Rajput* and *Ram Balram* to repay the debts he had incurred during the making of *Jaan Hazir Hai.* In the meantime, many events took place in Goldie's life.

He had not severed his connection with Rajneesh, and would reach the sets in the clothes he wore at the ashram. But an event made him move away from Rajneesh. In an argument between Parveen Babi and Mahesh Bhatt, Parveen Babi, in a fit of rage, had broken the necklace worn by Mahesh Bhatt with a photo of Rajneesh in it. The news somehow reached Rajneesh, who asked Vinod Khanna to summon Mahesh Bhatt.

'I made him what he is. I will destroy him now,' Rajneesh threatened.

Vinod Khanna met Mahesh Bhatt and asked him to meet Bhagwan (Rajneesh) in Pune and ask for his forgiveness. 'Else, he has threatened to destroy you,' Vinod added.

Mahesh Bhatt was a worried man. Goldie felt bad for Mahesh Bhatt but was also angry at Rajneesh's threat. How could a guru threaten to destroy his disciple, he wondered. It was the same Rajneesh who had once said that a true disciple could not live without his guru.

Rajneesh's comments about Mahesh Bhatt were enough to change Goldie's view about him. Whatever respect he had for him vanished that day.

A few days later it was Guru Purnima. Thousands of followers visited the ashram to meet Rajneesh. Goldie, too, went there. To his surprise, he found that Rajneesh was unwilling to give him any time. 'I am busy for the next fortnight,' he said, dismissing Goldie.

Goldie took off the necklace with the photo of Rajneesh and handed it to him, saying, 'I came to say convey my gratitude. You had once said that when the wings are strong, the bird flies out of the nest. I, too, have flown the roost. If you wish to speak to me, let me know, and I will make myself available.'

The next day Rajneesh began his discourse talking of Goldie. But he was done with Rajneesh and left for Bombay. A chapter in his life had ended.

The film industry's reactions were quite varied. While some welcomed him back, a few thought he was foolish to have wasted five years of his life. Dev Anand felt the same. He did not change his view about this even later. He spoke of how Goldie used to believe that Rajneesh entered Buddha's consciousness when he retired for the night. Dev had trashed such ideas. 'I went to the ashram once. Everyone except Rajneesh recognized me. Rajneesh was arrogant and ignored me,' Dev recalled the incident. He was upset that his brother had wasted precious years of his life, but Goldie believed it was part of his spiritual growth. He believed that no experience in life was a waste.

Goldie never met Rajneesh again. Nor did he speak ill of him ever. He believed that Rajneesh was his spiritual teacher and that he had learnt a lot from him.

It was unfortunate that yet another guru had turned out to be a fraud. But Goldie felt liberated that he had realized this in time and not stuck there forever. He realized that he could not depend on others for his growth and that he had to be his own teacher. He started believing that God was a part of him. But he never expressed his thoughts to others. He was at peace with himself now and did not aspire for anything desperately. He used to speak of his earlier life as if describing a previous birth. His past was like a dream for him.

❖❖❖

After the Rajneesh episode, Mahesh Bhatt introduced Goldie to the philosopher, U.G. Krishnamurti. But Goldie was now not keen to accept anyone as his guru. He did become friends with the philosopher and respected his views. In fact, U.G. was instrumental in getting Sushma and Goldie together.

Goldie, separated from Loveleen, had come to the conclusion that he could not forget Sushma. He had married Loveleen to forget Sushma. Sushma, too, having rejected Goldie's proposal, had not been able to marry anyone else. She was still unmarried. After returning from Pune, Goldie and Sushma started meeting each other often. Sushma would often accompany Goldie on his visits to U.G. The philosopher could guess that the two were in love.

One day Krishnamurti's daughter and son-in-law were visiting him in Bombay. The flat where U.G. stayed had been given away by him to Parveen Babi. Krishnamurti's son-in-law was an astrologer. He told Sushma and Goldie,

'In South of India, an uncle can marry his niece. That is, a man can marry his elder sister's daughter but not of the younger sister. In fact, these marriages take place to ensure that the property remains within the family. Why are you both hesitating?'

U.G. too encouraged the two. Sushma and Goldie, now encouraged, started thinking seriously of marriage. Sushma consulted her brother's wife, who was from South India, and she agreed that such a marriage was possible.

They both decided to go ahead with their plans. On 12 March, 1978, the marriage took place in the presence of close family members. Sushma's mother remained opposed to the marriage and did not attend.

The couple took the blessings of Chetan Anand after the wedding. Luckily, he did not oppose. But Dev Anand was furious. So were Goldie's sisters. They decided to cut off their relations with Goldie.

Time flew. Sushma and Goldie had settled down when he started getting new offers. After the success of *Dream Girl,* Hema Malini's secretary Indra Kumar Behl approached Goldie for a new movie in 1978. Behl had decided to cast Dharmendra opposite Hema. They both were a pair in reel and in real life. Their romance was the industry's gossip. It was Dharmendra who suggested Goldie's name. Behl knew Goldie formally. Goldie demanded a fee of ₹40 lakhs for the movie; Behl immediately agreed. The movie was *Ek Do Teen Chaar.*

The story and screenplay were written by Goldie. Dev Anand, Raakhee, Hema Malini, Dharmendra, Parveen Babi, Shashi Kapoor, Tina Munim and Rishi Kapoor completed the star cast for this multi-starrer with four heroes and four heroines. It was an extension of a love triangle where each person loved someone else. The music was being composed by Pancham. One song was recorded in Lata Mangeshkar's voice.

Suiting the grand scale of the movie, the *muhurat* too was planned in Mehboob Studio. The scene for the *muhurat* was that of the four heroines being kidnapped by the villain and the four heroes coming to their rescue. The set for the shooting had been created spending nearly ₹5.5 lakhs. Behl was keen to shoot at a foreign locale. Goldie visited a few foreign locations but when he returned, he heard that Hema Malini and Behl had some differences of opinion and that Hema had terminated his job. Goldie believed it was a matter of money. Hema complained to Goldie of Behl having cheated her.

Apparently, Behl had borrowed some money from the producer without Hema's knowledge. Hema's mother Jaya Chakravarthy was upset at Behl's behaviour. Seeing a lot of problems ahead, Goldie thought it best to drop the movie altogether.

Goldie knew that his sisters were not happy with his marriage to Sushma but he knew that most people mellowed down when a child was born into the family. Within two years, Vaibhav was born, and the families came together once more. Goldie and Sushma were now enjoying a lovely family along with a blessed married life.

❖❖❖

The Ramsay brothers made most of their horror-genre movies at Goldie's Ketnav studios. Goldie stayed in a flat on these premises. He would attend many trials of the movies screened at Ketnav and thought the films made by the Ramsay brothers technically superior. Goldie was impressed by their focused approach. They were always seen doing their editing, dubbing and other such tasks diligently. The brothers narrated a few scripts to Goldie with a view to having him on board as a director, but he did not like any of them. Also, Goldie felt that the banner needed someone else to be the director.

Goldie came up with a story and script of his own, and suggested, 'I will act in the movie as I suit the role. We can take Rekha as the heroine.'

Those days Rekha was a close friend of Goldie. She would visit him very often and, if they met on the road, she would shout 'Goldie!' and rush to hug him. Sushma treated Rekha as a member of their family. On hearing the script for *Ghunghroo Ki Awaaz,* Rekha readily agreed to do the film.

The story was about a wealthy landlord who had no family. He led a sad life, completely trusting his uncle who stayed with him. The landlord, already in depression, becomes further ill when his uncle starts mixing some drugs with his medicines. The uncle's devious plans were to take over the properties on his death. A nurse is appointed to take care of the young man, who falls in love with her. Little does he know that the nurse in hand in glove with the uncle and they stage a plot where the young man fires his gun at her. He loses his mental balance when he realizes that he may be apprehended for murder. The uncle advises him to run away. While being treated in a government hospital, he sees the same nurse again. The nurse is now repentant. The young man realizes that it was his uncle who played the game all along. He confronts his uncle, '*Mama* (maternal uncle) has two ma's in it but you never realized the power of that word.'

The Ramsay brothers, in their typical style, had incorporated a few horror scenes. Goldie behaved like a professional actor, never interfering in their work.

In a few scenes Goldie is shown hugging Rekha but their intimate touch was not of sensuality but that of affection and love, like a child hugging his mother. Before a particularly intimate scene, Rekha suddenly refused, saying she felt uncomfortable. Goldie tried explaining to her that the scene was an integral part of the script and that it demanded such an intimate moment. Goldie decided to rewrite some of the scenes seeing Rekha's adamancy.

Rekha started misbehaving. She once went away to Madras without informing anyone, disturbing the schedule by nearly two months. She put conditions that she would not work beyond a shift. She had stopped talking to Goldie for anything other than work-related matters. Goldie was surprised. Earlier, Rekha would share all her problems with him but now she had become difficult to work with.

The main reason for her erratic behaviour was her love affair with Amitabh Bachchan. Amitabh would call while she was on the sets and they would talk for hours together. As per Tulsi Ramsay, it was Amitabh who had asked Rekha not to do any intimate scenes. Tulsi also believed that Rekha was not happy with the fact that though Goldie had signed up with another producer as a writer-director, he was not inclined to give the lead role to her. Goldie did not feel the role suited Rekha. It is a different matter that the movie was never shot. But Rekha's behaviour led to the production of *Ghunghroo Ki Awaaz* suffering badly, not to mention a lot of headaches for Goldie.

The Ramsay brothers were being tossed around while the cold war between Rekha and Goldie continued. Goldie would expect them to get Rekha to agree for a scene. On the other hand, Rekha would give her own comments on how a scene should be shot! She told them one day, 'Romance is expressed through the eyes. One need not be physical to express these emotions. Have you not seen Bimal Roy movies?'

'Madam, we have seen all. But this script demands that you are physically close to the patient. A madman does not know how to do romance. He hugs the nurse out of fear,' Tulsi tried explaining.

But Rekha was unwilling to listen.

The Ramsay brothers were in a dilemma. They were worried that Rekha would walk away in a huff if they argued. They would even get her favourite Sindhi kadhi to please her – but that too did not help! She stopped coming to the sets and demanded her payment. Goldie had promised her ₹3 lakhs for the movie, and the last installment of ₹80,000 was pending. Goldie refused to pay her the balance amount as she had refused to come for the dubbing. Rekha filed a complaint with the Cine and TV Artists' Association. Goldie, in turn, filed a case against her in the court. This was when Rekha agreed for a compromise and allowed Goldie to use a double for the remaining scenes and for the dubbing. She did not demand the balance payment either.

Goldie was desperate to finish the shooting, and took the help of Padma Khanna and others for the title song of *Ghungroo Ki Awaaz* and other scenes. He asked the dance director to teach Padma poses to make her resemble Rekha. Finally, the movie was ready.

But the news that the movie had been shot partly using duplicate artists for both acting and dubbing reached the distributors and they refused to promote the film. The news 'Vijay Anand in a soup' started doing the rounds and became the headlines in cine magazines. Obviously, the film flopped. Goldie's image as a hero was not strong enough to pull the movie through. The other character actors, like Dheeraj Kumar and Shriram Lagoo, too didn't have the appeal to attract crowds.

Goldie and Rekha were again paired together in Shekhar Kapur's *Time Machine*. Rekha had gone through a lot in the meanwhile. Her marriage was on the rocks. Goldie sympathized with her situation, but Rekha continued to behave formally, as if meeting him for the first time in her life.

❖❖❖

Someone from Delhi was ready to finance Chetan Anand's son Ketan's film. The story Ketan had chosen was that of two couples. He had a lot of respect for Goldie and wanted him to work on the film. Goldie agreed, and Ketan decided to cast Asha Parekh opposite Goldie. Ketan was in search of newcomers to play the younger couple. For some reasons the negotiations with the Delhi person failed and Ketan began pestering his father to produce the film and launch his career as a director. Chetan was already working on two films of his own and couldn't take up the financial burden of yet another film. When Goldie got to know of this, he asked Ketan, 'Why are you troubling your father? You know he is financially stuck. I will produce your film.'

Goldie had met Colonel Kapoor at Rajneesh Ashram and they had become good friends. Colonel Kapoor loved writing and Goldie had liked one of his short stories very much. A middle-class man sees his wife with her boss and he is so hurt that he tries committing suicide, but he survives and begins a new life.

Goldie tweaked this story and created a new story-screenplay with two generations. Once the dialogues were ready, he chose Shabana Azmi, Rehana Sultan and Kanwaljeet for the main roles. He himself was going to act in the film.

The young hero is shown in the first half of the film and in the second half the story of the aged hero's son is shown. The role of the young and the aged couple was played by Shabana and Goldie. The film was named *Hum Rahe Na Hum*. Goldie could think of none other than R.D. Burman to compose the music, but Ketan Anand preferred Bhappi Lahiri. Bappi Lahiri had composed the music for Sushma's brother Bhisham's film *Chalte Chalte,* and the songs were big hits. Goldie, too, had liked the music.

The shooting of *Hum Rahe Na Hum* began in 1980 and Goldie helped Ketan with the direction. Since he had written the screenplay, Goldie knew the dialogues of all the characters well. He would say each dialogue and measure the length with a stop watch, and tell Ketan how long a scene would be. Goldie could visualize the film in 3D (three-dimensional). On paper, every story is in 2D and the storywriter and the reader have two different perspectives; in a film, the viewer, writer and director come together and the viewer is not given time to think while watching the film.

Goldie's *Ghunghroo Ki Awaaz* was in progress at the same time and since Goldie was acting in it, *Hum Rahe Na Hum* took two years to complete. Since Goldie was not very popular as an actor, it was difficult to sell a film with him as the hero. The distributors refused to pay the price Goldie was demanding for his film. Hence, the film released only in Bombay and later it came out as video cassettes; elsewhere, it remained an unreleased film.

❖❖❖

It had been Dev Anand's lifelong dream to be known as a great filmmaker. He wanted to be known as a better director than Goldie and also other great filmmakers of the time. If Dev Anand and Goldie made films for Navketan, there was a danger of an unintentional competition and rivalry cropping up between them. So Goldie decided that it was better that he made films the way he wanted to, rather than compete with Dev Papa.

In reality, the films directed by Dev didn't do too well. Dev showed the films he made to Goldie before they released, though Goldie was not making films for Navketan now. Earlier, Dev used to show Goldie the rough rushes and would reshoot them based on Goldie's feedback. If Goldie made some specific comments, Dev would refuse to accept them open-mindedly. He stopped showing Goldie the rushes of his films after *Hare Rama Hare Krishna*. Goldie got a chance to see them only when the re-recording had been completed. Dev would listen to Goldie's feedback but could clearly do nothing about them or make any changes. Once Goldie realized this, he stopped giving any suggestions. And soon, Dev stopped showing him the films altogether. Once in a while, he would ask Goldie,

'Do you want to see a trial?'

Goldie never went for the trial screenings as he knew the request didn't mean much. Goldie saw Dev's films only during the premiere show.

Goldie had very clear opinions about the films Dev made. He felt that Dev didn't have a very deep understanding about original stories and he made films on very superficial and shallow subjects. That was why his films lacked depth. Goldie felt that Dev looked at films from an actor's point of view. This was the case not only with Dev but any actor who produced or directed films. Dev Anand as a director never forgets Dev Anand as an actor when he makes a film. Quite naturally, the story tends to revolve around the actor.

Goldie believed that other actors aped Dev. That was because Dev would enact the scenes before the shot, and all actors, be it the actress, villain or even the character actor playing the role of the hero's father, would start aping him. Goldie felt it was important for a filmmaker to be able to mix with everyone naturally. This was impossible for Dev, who could never forget his image. He had kept himself in a cocoon and had start looking outdated. The real world was that of the viewers but Dev never believed in seeing a movie in a theatre. It was important for a filmmaker to see the reaction of the viewers. They may laugh during a scene that the filmmaker had intended to be poignant.

Dev lived the screen image of fifty years in his real life too. Goldie felt Dev had hidden his personal life from others, giving a lot of importance to his film persona. He would always be well dressed, wearing a buttoned-up shirt with a scarf even in the heat of Bombay summers. No one had seen him in a simple kurta-pyjama. He would never answer the door, lest the visitor saw him in his home dress. It was rumoured that he would go abroad for plastic surgery each year. But Goldie dismissed them as mere rumours. People always wondered about Dev's ever-lasting energy and youthful face. But they didn't know the amount of effort Dev took to maintain that. He led an extremely disciplined life. He had given up lunch at the age of fifty-five. He would have water and an apple in the morning and drink fruit juice in the evening. He would work till midnight. After dinner, he would walk for half an hour with a stick in hand. He never missed his morning workout. He took care of his hair. He would not leave his make-up room till his hair was in place. He was not addicted to anything. At parties, people would throng around him, clamouring to give him a glass of alcohol. He would never refuse a drink, picking up the glass but never drinking from it. He would quietly keep the glass of whiskey or wine on a table after a while. If asked, he would again pick up another glass to keep it back later! Dev knew that the signs of alcohol would show on his face, so he stayed away from it. None of the three Anand brothers could handle alcohol as it led to upset stomachs. They all stayed away from it.

The publicity machinery had often accused Dev of being an ordinary actor but Goldie always maintained that he was a fine actor with some limitations. Goldie felt there was no one as good-looking as Dev, and he had always taken care not to be in maudlin scenes or where he was laughing out loud. The audience, too, did not appreciate sentimental scenes of Dev and would laugh in the theatres. It was not the viewers' fault – Dev did not know how to do such scenes with authenticity. Though a sensitive person, Dev never expressed his emotions freely, preferring to shed his tears behind closed doors. He just didn't know how to express his emotions on screen openly. Dev worked hard to maintain his image as someone who did not dwell in the past or worry about the future; he always lived in the present.

There probably isn't anyone as hard-working as Dev or one who has devoted his entire life to the film industry. Goldie had a lot of differences with Dev on various issues but he loved him dearly till the end. Goldie wished Dev would break free from his image. He was of the opinion that an actor who worked for many years should know how to break away from his image.

Goldie sincerely wanted a movie directed by Dev to be a hit. But he knew that it was possible only when Dev changed his storywriter and was willing to listen to the story and scriptwriter. (Goldie's wish remained a wish forever).

After *Bullet,* Dev didn't work with Goldie, but they came together thanks to Dev Anand's son Suneil Anand. The father-son duo had been introduced to the world through *Anand Aur Anand*. But the movie flopped at the box office and Dev was in search of another story to give Suneil's career a boost. Goldie readily agreed to make a movie for Suneil. After all, Suneil was his nephew!

In *Main Tere Liye,* directed by Goldie, Suneil's co-star was Meenakshi Seshadri. Normally, any movie by Goldie would create a buzz among distributors but this movie did not do so. Prem Prakash, Goldie's assistant, believed that the movie did not have Goldie's 'touch', though he could not put a finger on what exactly was missing. To add to it, Suneil was not hero material, and had not developed his personality as a star. His acting skills were limited and Goldie had to coach him for every shot. Thanks to his training in martial arts, he could do the fight scenes quite well. Goldie had been careful about the budget for the movie and cut corners wherever possible. His approach was very different from Dev's who, if someone asked for cola, would order a whole truck!

Goldie demanded ₹25 lakhs from the distributors for each territory. No one agreed, and Goldie was forced to reduce his demand to ₹10 lakhs, but by then there began the buzz about the movie being too ordinary and no one agreed even to the reduced amount. Finally, the movie was never screened. Dev blamed Goldie's stubbornness for the consequences.

❖❖❖

A new problem presented itself around this time. Vinod Khanna had quit Rajneesh Ashram in the US and returned to India. He and Goldie had developed a close friendship in Pune. Goldie would find Vinod crying after the meditation classes. Goldie once saw him sobbing like a child and patted his back to comfort him. Vinod would take Goldie's advice on various issues. Vinod had a lot of respect for Goldie but, surprisingly, had played games with him while shooting for *Rajput*. Vinod believed that when Goldie and Mahesh Bhatt quit the ashram, Goldie had insulted Rajneesh. He was very upset with Goldie and considered himself Rajneesh's true disciple and followed the guru to the United States. When things became difficult in the US with the government breathing down Rajneesh's neck, Vinod returned to India. He called Goldie upon landing. Goldie, as usual, did not keep Vinod's earlier behaviour in mind.

Vinod was silent when he met Goldie. After a while, he burst out sobbing. Goldie patiently allowed him to. He suggested, 'Vinod, why don't we meet some other day.'

Vinod met him after a few days and they walked up to the terrace. Vinod started crying once more. Goldie advised Vinod that he needed to start working.

There had been a criminal case registered at Rajneesh Ashram in the US and Vinod had run away in the fear that he may get embroiled in it. Vinod was not sure if he would be accepted in the film world and how the audience would react to his movies. His self-confidence was extremely low.

But Goldie assured him that he would do his best to launch him again. Goldie's moral support relaxed Vinod a bit. Goldie knew Vinod had been at the height of his career when he left

India. Many believe that had he not left then, he would have become a superstar. Even after returning from America, he was as handsome and fit as before; he was hero material. Goldie felt he could, as a friend and guide, help Vinod make a comeback. Keeping that in mind, he wrote a story for him.

The story was about Krishna and Arjun. Goldie wanted to cast Vinod as Arjun. He wanted a more mature actor for the role of Krishna, who would dispense advice and be a guide. Goldie thought of Dilip Kumar for the role of a modern Krishna. The idea was to match the wisdom of Krishna with the actions of Arjun.

'How are you? We must do something together,' Dilip Kumar would tell Goldie whenever they met. He would praise Goldie's acting whenever he saw his movie.

Goldie believed the earlier project had failed because Dilip Kumar did not want to work with Dev. Taking a chance, Goldie met Dilip Kumar at the Arts Club in Bandra. They both were members there and frequented the club often. Dilip Kumar would often sit there watching the sunset. Those days Dilip Kumar was busy shooting for Subhash Ghai's *Vidhaata*. As always, Dilip Kumar received Goldie affectionately and ordered his usual samosa and chai.

'Yusuf bhai, shall we make a movie together?'

'Haven't I said that before? I would love to!'

'There are two roles: one for you and the other for Vinod Khanna,' Goldie explained.

'I am making Vidhaata with Subhash Ghai. *Par ek gal hai, main dasriyatanu* prime role *mera hona chahiye,*' he said in Punjabi. 'I don't care about the number of scenes, but the story should revolve around me. Let Vinod Khanna sing songs or have fight scenes.'

'The story is titled *Krishna Arjun*. No one can say Arjun was greater than Krishna. I am looking at you for the role of Krishna. It will be a central role. No one will be a bigger fool than me if I were to give Vinod Khanna a role more crucial than yours,' Goldie assured Dilip Kumar.

Goldie continued after a while, 'Vinod Khanna wants to return to the industry. He is a friend and I am helping him. If you give me your dates, I can start the shooting immediately and finish it as fast as possible.'

Goldie and Dilip Kumar decided to meet once to discuss the story. When they met, Dilip Kumar listened to the story intently, asking Goldie to slow down his narration, asking him many questions along the way. Goldie wanted to move fast as the narration demanded speed but either Dilip Kumar's receptive power had reduced or his style was such, to listen slowly.

'It is a fantastic story but don't you think it needs to be loosened a bit to allow for good acting?' Dilip Kumar asked.

'Yusuf bhai, if performance comes in the way of storytelling, it is not performance anymore. My narrative will move well, including songs and fight sequences. Don't worry about that.'

Dilip Kumar seemed satisfied and asked Goldie to check with his secretary, John, for the dates. He knew Goldie since childhood and came to the point directly. He asked, 'How much will you pay me?'

'Whatever you want,' Goldie replied.

Dilip Kumar wanted Goldie to ask Subhash Ghai the amount he was paying. Goldie found that a little odd. Why would he ask someone else when he could hear it from Yusuf bhai himself? Finally, Dilip Kumar told him the amount, which Goldie agreed to immediately.

They both agreed to start the movie as soon as possible.

Surprisingly, after the meeting, Goldie kept calling Dilip Kumar to no avail. Dilip Kumar avoided taking the calls, and even picked up the phone once or twice to say in a false voice, 'Dilip Kumar is not at home'. Goldie could, of course, recognize that it was Dilip Kumar at the other end. Why was he avoiding him, Goldie wondered. More than a month passed by but Dilip Kumar didn't turn up. In the meanwhile, Vinod Khanna had signed up a couple of movies.

Goldie used to be a close friend of Saira Banu, Dilip

Kumar's wife. She had worked in the Dev Anand-starrer, *Pyar Mohabbat,* directed by Shankar Mukherjee. Saira admired Goldie's talent. After seeing *Tere Mere Sapne,* she had asked Dilip Kumar to watch it. Goldie called her one day to tell her about the movie he had planned with her husband.

'Yes, he told me about it. He said the story was very good. He was full of praise for it,' Saira said.

'I wonder why he has not responded for the past two months despite my repeated efforts. Does he not intend to do the movie with me? I wouldn't mind if that's so. But it isn't fair to keep me waiting while Vinod Khanna's dates are going waste. I have respected him a lot since my childhood days and my request to him is to not treat me so unfairly,' Goldie blurted out.

Goldie wanted the ordeal of waiting to end. Luckily, Dilip Kumar called the next day itself and said,

'Yaar, I didn't know you were in a hurry to start the shooting. You know, my pace is much slower than yours. It would be better if you look for someone else.'

'Yusuf bhai, if you feel so, I will do that. Hopefully, we will work together some day. I know I cannot change my style. Once I decide on the script and other things, I try to finish off the shoots at the earliest. But I am giving you a breathing time of nine months. I know you normally complete a movie in two to three years. Please think about it.'

'You see, I am finishing Subhash's movie and then will be off to England. Then there is some other tour ...' Dilip Kumar continued, but Goldie cut him off mid-sentence. 'It's fine, Yusuf bhai. We will meet soon.'

The chapter was closed. Dilip Kumar knew Goldie would make the movie in his own way and not accommodate to suit his style. Goldie did not allow any interference in the direction and script. Undoubtedly, Goldie realised, Dilip Kumar was not comfortable with his approach.

Any other producer-director would have bent backwards to accommodate Dilip Kumar but not Goldie. Other directors would have hounded Dilip Kumar for his dates and hosted parties in his favour. Goldie was aware of such tricks. He had told producer Mushir once that making a movie with Dilip Kumar is like working for him. Mushir Alam later went on to be one of the producers of *Shakti,* which starred Dilip Kumar.

Goldie decided not to work with Dilip Kumar in the future. But, thankfully, Dilip Kumar continued to treat Goldie with respect whenever the two met.

Their next encounter happened when Dilip Kumar was directing *Kalinga.* Dilip Kumar was the vice-president of a trust run by Goldie. One day, after the meeting of the trustees, when everyone had left, Dilip Kumar said, 'I want to show you a movie. But keep it to yourself.'

It was surprising that he had asked Goldie, as people like Yash Chopra and Shakti Samanta – both close to Dilip Kumar- were also present at the meeting.

Goldie went to Ajanta theatre to see the trials of *Kalinga.* Subhash Ghai was present, along with many others who had nothing to do with the movie. After the trials, Goldie was a little disturbed and Subhash Ghai looked rattled. They both wondered how they would be able to give a candid feedback to Dilip Kumar.

Subhash Ghai wanted to excuse himself and not say anything.

'Subhash, Dilip Kumar is a very big man and thousands will be willing to come and give their feedback. But he has asked the two of us. It would be unfair on our part to lie. I am going to give my candid feedback,' Goldie said.

'I am keeping my views to myself,' Subhash Ghai replied. 'I respect him a lot and cannot be blunt. I cannot dare to. But I will be with you when you speak.'

A little later, Dilip Kumar came in and asked, 'How was the movie?'

Goldie reflected for a while and said, 'There is one major fault in the film. You must fix that. You must get a new editor and re-shoot some parts of the movie. The film is already over three and a half hours and will get to a length of nearly four hours. You must edit it to two and a half hours or less. And then you may add some scenes if you wish.'

He added, 'I can tell you which scenes to edit.'

Subhash Ghai nodded in agreement. They discussed for a few hours. While Goldie had been honest, he realized that it had hurt Dilip Kumar's ego. Goldie said while leaving, 'You may call me anytime and I would be happy to help in editing.'

Dilip Kumar saw Goldie and Subhash Ghai off at the door. Later, Goldie came to know through a recording artist working on the *Kalinga* project that Dilip Kumar had the editing team make all the changes suggested by Goldie. Unfortunately, the movie never saw the light of day as differences cropped up between producer Sudhakar Bokade and Dilip Kumar.

❖❖❖

Goldie was getting tired of the film industry. The industry, too, had changed a lot. Goldie felt that the actors and the technicians did not give their best. The shift system had started and actors would come in for a two-hour or a five-hour shift and then rush off to other sets. This bothered Goldie. He was receiving many offers but the drive to direct and write a story and a script was missing. He was not willing to tolerate star tantrums anymore. He decided to move away from the film industry. After his marriage to Sushma and the birth of his son, he was a contented man. Goldie stayed away from the industry for the next five or six years. The only thing he did in the meantime was direct two episodes of Chetan Anand's TV serial *Param Vir Chakra*.

But the acting bug had never left him completely! It was in 1991-92 that Shekhar Kapur came to meet him and offered him the lead role in a television serial.

Earlier Goldie had acted in Shekhar Kapur's *Time Machine,* which was left incomplete. Goldie had thoroughly enjoyed acting in it. He could not refuse Shekhar Kapur's offer and shot two episodes. Unfortunately, Doordarshan did not clear the same in time. In the meanwhile, Shekhar Kapur got busy with the shooting of *Phoolan Devi.* The task of directing the television serial, *Tehkikaat,* was given to Karan Razdan. As it happened, Razdan fell ill after shooting a few episodes, and the responsibility fell on Goldie. Doordarshan, seeing the serial's popularity, granted an extension and it was left to Goldie to complete the project.

❖❖❖

The itch to make a movie would surface once a while. Goldie had a few scripts in mind. While visiting the sets of *1942: A Love Story* at Goregaon Film City in 1992, Goldie concluded that producer-director Vidhu Vinod Chopra was a talented young man. Anil Kapoor, who was on the sets, asked Goldie why he had stopped making movies.

'I don't like the shift system.'

'I don't work in shifts like others. My father was a film producer and I understand the constraints. Why don't you plan a movie?' Anil Kapoor proposed.

'I can but there should be a proper share of profit when the movie succeeds. I will ensure that we have a fine script.'

Anil Kapoor agreed. Goldie had in mind a story with two heroes but first wanted to ensure that Anil Kapoor did not object to working with another hero. He suggested the name of Jackie Shroff. When Goldie met Jackie, he was excited to work on the project. Goldie appreciated the fact that both the youngsters showed a lot of respect for him and were eager to prove their talent.

Goldie had a habit of watching the movies of the actors he was signing for his movie. He would make a note of their talent, writing down their strengths and weaknesses. It was important for him to develop the character accordingly. He would try and understand why a particular movie failed or succeeded.

After watching nearly ten movies of Anil Kapoor and Jackie Shroff, Goldie was ready with a script within a week.

Goldie asked Anil Kapoor and Jackie Shroff to come for a reading of the script. Despite confirming the time, Anil Kapoor did not turn up. He didn't even bother to inform Goldie of his change of plans. This happened a few times; when Goldie called, Anil Kapoor would give some lame excuse of being busy elsewhere.

One day, to Goldie's surprise, he found that Anil Kapoor was travelling to Ooty when they were supposed to meet. An incensed Goldie rang up Anil Kapoor at Ooty.

'Anil, this is ridiculous. If you are not interested in doing the movie, please tell me so, but don't make a fool of me. I have many other things to tie up and I cannot have you telling me at the last moment that you didn't like the script.'

Anil Kapoor assured him of meeting soon. In the meanwhile, Goldie met Bappi Lahiri for the music and got eight songs recorded. He signed Juhi Chawla and Raveena Tandon as female leads.

He went ahead with the *muhurat* shot. There too Anil Kapoor and Jackie Shroff were absent. Anil Kapoor's secretary Rikku Rakesh Nath was present though and promised that Anil Kapoor would meet Goldie soon. Juhi Chawla and Raveena Tandon were present and Goldie gave a signing amount to each of the stars.

Goldie decided to read the script to Jackie but the experience there too was similar to that of Anil Kapoor. Jackie would defer the appointment, saying he would make himself available when Anil was present. One day a frustrated Goldie called Jackie's wife Ayesha and asked whether Jackie was willing to work without Anil Kapoor. Ayesha assured that Jackie was keen to work and that he respected Goldie a lot.

While Jackie's secretary also kept assuring Goldie, Jackie never called Goldie.

Goldie realized that he had wasted three months in the hope of getting the movie off the ground. Perhaps Anil had, in a fit of emotion, agreed to do the movie but developed cold feet later. Goldie did not want to waste time and money starting the project only to be shelved later. He then used a trade publication to announce that he had dropped plans for the movie. Luckily, he had taken a token one rupee from the distributors, so he did not have any debts to be repaid.

Anil Kapoor's reply to Goldie was a white lie. He claimed that he had never promised Goldie, and that Goldie had merely asked whether he was keen on doing a movie together. Goldie deemed it below his dignity to argue. He felt sad that Anil Kapoor, who addressed him as uncle, had now to decided to move to greener pastures. They preferred to work with popular and successful directors like David Dhawan rather than act in a sensitively directed film by Goldie.

Goldie conducted screen tests with new actors. Juhi Chawla and Raveena Tandon had been patient and supported Goldie all the way. Unfortunately, Goldie had to drop the project when he could not find the right talent for his movie.

❖❖❖

Goldie may have dropped the film, but filmmaking was far from over for him. Producer Roshan Wadhera had met Goldie while he was working in *Tehkikaat;* they had known each other for nearly four decades. When he met Goldie, he was producing *Tum Jiyo Hazaron Saal* with distribution support from the National Film Development Corporation of India (NFDC). Wadhera had developed good relations with NFDC chief Ravi Gupta and they had decided to work on another movie. This is where Wadhera wanted Goldie's help.

Wadhera had a good script in hand, and he truly believed only Goldie could do justice to it. Wadhera was not only a friend of Goldie's, but also a fan of his direction and films. Ravi Gupta, too, respected Goldie a lot.

Wadhera had a Bengali script, which was based on Julia Roberts' *Dying Young*.

'I am not in favour of adapting Hollywood movies. I prefer to work in my own way when it comes to writing and direction. I have a good story and we can discuss that if you are interested,' Goldie countered.

Wadhera liked the story when he heard it and asked Goldie to work on the script. The story of *Nyayamurti Krishnamurthy* was that of an upright judge. Goldie put a condition that he would act in the title role. Wadhera had given his sister's son Sandeep Kapoor a break in *Tum Jiyo Hazaron Saal,* and was keen that he should get to work under a talented director like Goldie. Goldie had no objection to casting Sandeep as the hero.

The discussion veered to Goldie's remuneration. 'I will give you the profits from whichever territory you select,' he told Goldie.

Goldie took a token ₹31,000 as signing amount. The news of Goldie getting back into film production spread all over, and many aspiring actors queued up to try their luck. Arun Irani, Prem Chopra and a few others called on Goldie directly, asking him if they could have a chance in his film. Wadhera expressed his concern to Aruna Irani about his inability to pay her the amount as per her stature. But Aruna Irani was not bothered about the sum. She just wanted to work with Goldie. Wadhera had a modest budget of less than ₹2 crores.

In fact, he paid some actors a mere ₹1000. Actress Simran, who had just made her debut, was chosen as the female lead.

Goldie settled on the popular music duo of Dilip Sen-Sameer Sen. Indeevar was the lyricist and, as was his style, Goldie wrote the opening lines of the song *Mera ek sapna*. They recorded the song, sung by Udit Narayan and Anuradha Paudwal, in Sahara studio at Goregaon, along with a theme song.

A grand *muhurat* took place at Centaur hotel. The film industry was abuzz with the news 'Goldie returns to film industry with *Nyayamurti Krishnamurthy,* giving Wadhera and the movie a lot of publicity. The function was attended by many industry stalwarts.

The shooting began in right earnest, with a few scenes of the song *Mera Koi Sapna Hai* being shot. A few music companies had been in touch with Wadhera for the music rights. Jayantilal Gada of Pen Music had come with a cheque of ₹5 lakhs. He was willing to pay ₹50,000 for the music rights. When consulted, Goldie advised, 'Don't give the rights to Pen Music. I will get someone else who is willing to pay ₹80 lakhs lakhs. You return the cheque he has given you.'

As the shooting began, Goldie found that the advisory committee of NFDC had found some objections in the script.

Ravi Gupta told Wadhera on the phone, 'A few members are not happy with the script. They feel that it has a few things against the government and its judiciary.' As NFDC was part of the ministry, it could not approve a script which criticized the government. Wadhera discussed the issue with Goldie, who challenged, 'Who right does NFDC have to change my script? I will not allow even a word to be changed.'

Ravi Gupta was taken aback by Goldie's stand, but promised Wadhera he would discuss this with the board. He also explained that certain changes would be unavoidable. But soon NFDC sent a letter stating they were unable to proceed as Goldie was unwilling to accept any changes. By then Wadhera had already spent nearly ₹14 lakhs. Without the funding from NFDC, it was impossible to shoot further. Ravi Gupta resigned without any notice about that time. The movie was in doldrums now. For nearly two years, NFDC remained headless and both *Tum Jiyo Hazaron Saal* and *Nyayamurti Krishnamurthy* remained incomplete.

A dejected Goldie focused on *Jaana Na Dil Se Door.* He did not know then that it would turn out to be his last movie.

❖❖❖

Chetan Anand was not just an elder brother to Goldie, but almost a father figure. Goldie had nursed him when he was ill. Goldie would sit with him for hours, talking to him and giving him company. When Chetan died in 1996, it affected Goldie badly; it took him many years to get over the tragedy.

Before Chetan's death, all the three brothers had decided to make a movie together. Goldie wanted to dedicate the movie to Chetan and that was how the idea for *Jaana Na Dil Se Door* came up. Goldie was admitted to Lilavati Hospital for a heart problem, but he declined to get a bypass surgery done as advised by the doctors. He had a lot of faith in homeopathy and took medicines prescribed by a homeopath in Kolkata. His health did improve but he had a lot of diet restrictions. He was weak and unable to take a lot of mental or physical stress. But he was not willing to give up his plans for the movie.

Keeping some parts of Chetan's personality in mind, Goldie had scripted a sensitive story about a father and his daughter. Goldie wanted Dev Papa to do the role of the father. He wanted to sign Manisha Koirala and Aamir Khan, but Manisha declined, saying she had already committed her time elsewhere. Perhaps Manisha was not comfortable with doing the double role of a daughter and wife to Dev Anand. Goldie decided to cast a newcomer, Indrani Banerjee, for the role. She had debuted with Prakash Mehra's *Dalaal*. Realizing that a star like Aamir Khan may not agree when the main role was that of Dev Anand's, Goldie decided to offer the role to a newcomer.

He soon zeroed in on Vikram from Delhi, who was willing to learn sincerely. The shooting began. Goldie had given Vikram the screen name Rajeshwar.

Dev was working with Goldie after a long time but his experience was not satisfactory. Dev told the author that while Goldie was putting in a lot of effort, the director in him was dead. He candidly admitted that the sensitivity Goldie showed while directing his films was lost after he had returned from Rajneesh's ashram.

Before the completion of the movie, there were offers for overseas rights and for different territories in India but Goldie was adamant on a particular amount and none of the distributors agreed. Producers make money only when distributors buy the prints. Due to Goldie's attitude, the prints were not sold and the film was never released. Goldie suffered a lot on this account but he maintained his stand about the payment.

There is a new trend of releasing movies as a 'world premiere'. This is especially true for movies that never get a release in theatres or flop at the box office. A few channels were ready for the world premiere of *Jaana Na Dil Se Door* but Goldie was not agreeable to the idea and refused.

❖❖❖

While Goldie was going through these challenges, two events occurred that affected him both physically and mentally. One was the murder of Priya Rajvansh, Chetan Anand's partner. The police arrested Chetan's sons Ketan and Vivek as suspects in the murder. The murder had apparently taken place due to a property dispute.

Goldie was the executor of Chetan's will. He tried his best to get Ketan and Vivek released on bail, and as executor of the will he had to make many court appearances. Dev Anand was busy with his work and had kept himself away from these matters from the beginning. But Goldie could not leave Chetan's sons to their fate. He tried his best to get bail for his nephews.

They say good things emerge from bad events. Thanks to the tragedy, Goldie was able to meet Chetan's former wife Uma Anand-Chatterjee. While *Hum Dono* was being shot, she had left home, saying she was visiting her parents but had stayed at Ebrahim Alkazi's house. Later, they both got married. Goldie loved Uma didi a lot. Hurt by the fact that she had lied, Goldie had promised himself never to meet or talk to her again. When Uma came to know of her sons being arrested, she visited Bombay.

She told Goldie, 'I know I told a lie when I left and that it has hurt you a lot. I considered you my son and now when I see you acting like a parent for my sons, I feel you are their guardian. You are, in some sense, redeeming the love you got from me by helping my sons.'

Goldie was touched by her words. The angst he held for so many years had been washed away.

While Goldie was yet to recover from the murder investigation, he was called by the ruling Bharatiya Janata Party to take charge as the censor board chief. He was a supporter of the BJP, and while he personally did not have any positive views about the censor board, he thought he could contribute to bridging the gap between the board and the industry. He accepted the offer. He was aware of the lackadaisical attitude of many board members who would not attend the screening, and also the arrogance of many members in the way they treated filmmakers with disdain. Goldie tried his best to reduce such misunderstandings and felt that he was contributing to the film industry. But he had to resign on differences of opinion with then Information and Broadcasting minister Sushma Swaraj. The minster believed that nude films needed to be screened in different theaters. Goldie did not believe in bending to someone else's views and resigned promptly. He had no attraction for the perks that came with the post, though he was criticized when he resigned. He was not in good health and small ailments seemed to be troubling him every now and then.

Shortly after his resignation, Goldie got a chance to head a TV channel called Lamhaz. It was a challenging role in the changing world of television and Goldie gladly accepted the offer. For various reasons, there were doubts whether the channel would take off; Goldie decided to quit and not spoil his name and the careers of many who would have joined the channel based on his trust alone.

❖❖❖

Goldie was talented, intelligent, innocent. Yet, blunt, sensitive and a little adamant. Everyone, including actors and newcomers, who came in touch with him benefitted. He gave, but never bothered to receive. He would never have entered the film industry had it not been for Dev Anand, Chetan Anand and Uma didi. He would not have thought of living the life of an ascetic had he not met Rajneesh. He experienced what life threw at him. He had never been formally trained in filmmaking or scriptwriting. He believed in life experiences, and that one could understand the agony of separation only if one fell in love.

He wanted to use all his experiences to make one final movie. Despite facing many difficulties, he never compromised with the basic values he cherished. The sensitive director in him was finished after his stint with Rajneesh. He had lost his zeal and ambition too. Goldie, who firmly believed that one could change one's destiny, was unable to deflect the negative events he faced.

He had lived a life of despair for many years. He was detached and did not get excited easily or look forward to praise. Achievements had lost their meaning for him. But thanks to his son Vaibhav, who expressed a desire to join the film industry, Goldie's interest in films remained. Vaibhav was sent abroad to study filmmaking. Goldie had plans to launch him on his return. He wanted to introduce Vaibhav to the industry on his twenty-sixth marriage anniversary.

But fate had other things in store for him.

Goldie was shifted to the ICU of Ramkrishna Mission Hospital on 14 February, 2004; he was suffering from respiratory problems. He felt better after a couple of days and returned home only to be admitted to Lilavati Hospital next. Goldie left the world early on the morning of 23 February.

Goldie had made the careers of many, like Hema Malini, Premnath, Padma Khanna and others. But he never received the accolades he deserved. He had always maintained that he never regretted it, but the fact that he was not recognized continued to hurt him. Despite making many sensitive and top-rated movies, Goldie remained a non-entity. But Goldie was beyond all this now. His quest for life had stopped. In the words of Goldie:

Tan rahe na rahe, main rahoonga
Maut ek khayal hai
Jaise zindagi ek khayal hai
Na sukh hai, na dukh hai
Na din hai, na duniya hai
Na insaan hai, na bhagwan
Sirf main hoon, main hoon, aur main hoon
Sirf main hoon.

[The body may perish but I shall remain

Death is a mere thought
Likewise, life too
There is neither happiness nor sorrow
Neither day nor world
Neither man nor god
It is just me, me, and me alone
It is just me.]

Goldie's Filmography

Year and movie	– **1954 • Taxi Driver**
Producer	– Dev Anand
Story & Screenplay	– Vijay Anand
Director	– Chetan Anand
Actors	– Dev Anand, Kalpana Kartik, Johnny Walker
Music director	– Sachin Dev Burman

Year and movie	– **1955 • Joru Ka Bhai** (as actor)
Producer & Director	– Chetan Anand
Actors	– Balraj Sahni, Sheetal Ramani, Johnny Walker, Vijay Anand
Music director	– Jaidev

Year and movie	– **1947 • Nau Do Gyarah**
Producer	– Dev Anand
Director, Story & Screenplay	– Vijay Anand
Actors	– Dev Anand, Kalpana Kartik, Lalita Pawar, Sashikala, Jeevan
Music director	– S.D. Burman

Year and movie	–	**1947 • Agra Road** (as actor)
Producer & Director	–	Ravindra Dave
Actors	–	Shakeela, Vijay Anand, Bhagwan, Nanda
Music director	–	Roshan

Year and movie	–	**1960 • Kala Bazaar**
Producer	–	Navketan Films
Director, Story & Screenplay	–	Vijay Anand
Actors	–	Dev Anand, Waheeda Rahman, Nanda, Vijay Anand, Leela Chitnis
Music director	–	S.D. Burman

Year and movie	–	**1961 • Hum Dono**
Producer	–	Navketan Films
Story & Screenplay	–	Vijay Anand
Director	–	Amarjeet
Actors	–	Dev Anand, Sadhana, Nanda
Music director	–	Jaidev

Year and movie	–	**1963 • Tere Ghar Ke Saamne**
Producer	–	Navketan Films
Director, Story & Screenplay	–	Vijay Anand
Actors	–	Dev Anand, Nutan, Om Prakash, Rajendra Nath
Music director	–	S.D. Burman

Year and movie	**–**	**1964 • Haqeekat** (as actor)
Producer, Director, Story & Screenplay	–	Chetan Anand
Actors	–	Balraj Sahni, Dharmendra,
	–	Priya Rajvansh, Vijay Anand
Music director	–	Madan Mohan

Year and movie	**–**	**1965 • Guide**
Producer	–	Dev Anand
Director	–	Vijay Anand
Story & Screenplay	–	R.K. Narayan, Vijay Anand
Actors	–	Dev Anand, Waheeda Rehman, Kishore Sahu
Music director	–	S.D. Burman

Year and movie	**–**	**1966 • Teesri Manzil**
Producer & Story	–	Nasir Hussain
Director & Screenplay	–	Vijay Anand
Actors	–	Shammi Kapoor, Asha Parekh, Prem Chopra
Music director	–	Rahul Dev Burman

Year and movie	**–**	**1967 • Jewel Thief**
Producer	–	Navketan Films
Director & Screenplay	–	Vijay Anand
Story	–	A.K. Narayan
Actors	–	Dev Anand, Ashok Kumar, Vaijayanthimala
Music director	–	S.D. Burman

Year and movie	–	**1968 • Kahin Aur Chal**
Producer	–	Jal Mistry
Director, Story & Screenplay	–	Vijay Anand
Actors	–	Dev Anand, Asha Parekh, Shubha Khote
Music director	–	Shankar-Jaikishan

Year and movie	–	**1970 • Johnny Mera Naam**
Producer	–	Gulshan Rai
Director & Screenplay	–	Vijay Anand
Story	–	A.K. Narayan
Actors	–	Dev Anand, Hema Malini, I.S. Johar, Premnath
Music director	–	Kalyanji-Anandji

Year and movie	–	**1971 • Tere Mere Sapne**
Producer, Director & Screenplay	–	Vijay Anand
Story	–	Based on the novel written by A.J. Cronin
Actors	–	Dev Anand, Mumtaz, Hema Malini, Vijay Anand
Music director	–	S.D. Burman

Year and movie	–	**1972 • Double-Cross** (as actor)
Producer	–	Yash Kohli
Director & Screenplay	–	Vijay Anand
Story	–	Suraj Sanim
Actors	–	Vijay Anand, Rekha, Asha Sachdev
Music director	–	Rahul Dev Burman

Year and movie	– **1973 • Chupa Rustam**
Producer & Director	– Vijay Anand
Actors	– Dev Anand, Vijay Anand, Hema Malini, Premnath, Ajit
Music director	– S.D. Burman

Year and movie	– **1973 • Blackmail**
Producer	– Vinod Doshi
Director, Story & Screenplay	– Vijay Anand
Actors	– Dharmendra, Rakhee, Shatrughan Sinha, Madan Puri
Music director	– Kalyanji–Anandji

Year and movie	– **1973 • Hindustan Ki Kasam** (as actor)
Producer	– Ravi Anand
Director, Story & Screenplay	– Chetan Anand
Actors	– Rajkumar, Priya Rajvansh, Vijay Anand
Music director	– Madan Mohan

Year and movie	– **1974 • Kora Kagaz** (as actor)
Producer	– Sanat Kothari
Director	– Anil Ganguly
Actors	– Vijay Anand, Jaya Bhaduri, Achala Sachdev, A.K. Hangal
Music director	– Kalyanji-Anandji

Year and movie	–	**1974 • Chor Chor** (as actor)
Producer	–	Vijay Anand
Director	–	Prem Prakash
Actors	–	Vijay Anand, Iftikar, Leena Chandavarkar
Music director	–	Lakshmikant- Pyarelal

Year and movie	–	**1975 • Jaan Hazir Hai**
Producer	–	Vijay Anand
Director	–	Manharnath Rangru
Actors	–	Prem Kishan, Natasha, Shekhar Kapoor
Music director	–	Jaykumar Parte

Year and movie	–	**1976 • Bullet**
Producer & Director	–	Vijay Anand
Actors	–	Dev Anand, Parveen Babi, Kabir Bedi
Music director	–	Rahul Dev Burman

Year and movie	–	**1978 • Main Tulsi Tere Angan Ki** (as actor)
Producer & Director	–	Raj Khosla
Actors	–	Nutan, Asha Parekh, Vijay Anand, Vinod Khanna
Music director	–	Lakshmikant-Pyarelal

Year and movie	–	**1980 • Ram Balram**
Producer	–	Tito
Director & Screenplay	–	Vijay Anand
Story	–	Kamleshwar
Actors	–	Amitabh, Dharmendra, Zeenat Aman, Rekha
Music director	–	Lakshmikant-Pyarelal

Year and movie	–	**1981 • Ghungroo Ki Awaaz**
Producer, Story	–	Vijay Anand
Director	–	Tulsi Ramsay
Actors	–	Vijay Anand, Rekha, Dheeraj Kumar, Dr. Shreeram Lagoo
Music director	–	Rahul Dev Burman

Year and movie	–	**1982 • Rajput**
Producer	–	Mushir- Riyaz
Director, Story & Screenplay	–	Vijay Anand
Actors	–	Dharmendra, Rajesh Khanna, Tina Munim, Hema Malini
Music director	–	Lakshmikant-Pyarelal

Year and movie	–	**1984 • Hum Rahe Na Hum**
		Producer & Screenplay –
Vijay Anand		
Director	–	Ketan Anand
Story	–	Karnal Singh
Actors		Vijay Anand, Shabana Azmi, Rehana Sultan

Music director	–	Bhappi Lahiri

Year and movie	**–**	**1988 • Main Tere Liye**
Director	–	Vijay Anand
Actors	–	Sunil Anand, Meenakshi Sheshadri, Nutan, Rajendra Kumar
Music director	–	Bhappi Lahiri

Year and movie	**–**	**2001 • Jana Na Dil Se Dur**
Producer, Director, Story & Screenplay	–	Vijay Anand
Actors	–	Dev Anand, Rajeshwar, Indrani Banerjee
Music director	–	Dilip Sen – Sameer Sen